Shawn Kate Hersh

P9-CJT-313

Shawn Kate Hersh

Virginia's
HISTORIC HOMES & GARDENS

Virginia's
HISTORIC HOMES & GARDENS

Pat and Chuck Blackley

Voyageur Press

ON THE FRONT COVER: *Thomas Jefferson's Monticello, Charlottesville.*

ON THE BACK COVER: *The east front of George Washington's Mount Vernon at sunrise. Perennial garden and old well house at James Monroe's Ash Lawn–Highland, Charlottesville. Carved chimneybreast in the dining room at Gunston Hall, Mason Neck.*

ON THE SPINE: *Carved pineapple finial, a symbol of hospitality, atop the Shirley Plantation home, Charles City.*

ON THE FRONTISPIECE: *(clockwise from top left) octagonal-shaped cupola and weathervane on Mount Vernon; boxwood bowknot garden at the Woodrow Wilson Birthplace, Staunton; English armillary sphere in the east garden at Stratford Hall Plantation, Stratford; plasterwork carving of Apollo on the ceiling of the master chamber at Kenmore, Fredericksburg.*

ON THE TITLE PAGE: *Entry gate and central brick walkway of the terraced garden at Kenmore's rear side. (inset) Large central passage or hallway at Patrick Henry's Scotchtown, Beaverdam.*

First published in 2009 by Voyageur Press, an imprint of MBI Publishing Company and the Quayside Publishing Group, 400 First Avenue N, Suite 300, Minneapolis, MN 55401 USA

Copyright © 2009 by Pat and Chuck Blackley

All rights reserved. With the exception of quoting brief passages for the purposes of review, no part of this publication may be reproduced without prior written permission from the Publisher.

The information in this book is true and complete to the best of our knowledge. All recommendations are made without any guarantee on the part of the author or Publisher, who also disclaim any liability incurred in connection with the use of this data or specific details.

This publication has been prepared solely by MBI Publishing Company and is not approved or licensed by any other entity. We recognize that some words, model names, and designations mentioned herein are the property of the trademark holder. We use them for identification purposes only. This is not an official publication.

Voyageur Press titles are also available at discounts in bulk quantity for industrial or sales-promotional use. For details write to Special Sales Manager at MBI Publishing Company, 400 First Avenue N, Suite 300, Minneapolis, MN 55401 USA.

Library of Congress Cataloging-in-Publication Data

Blackley, Pat.
  Virginia's historic homes and gardens / Pat and Chuck Blackley.
    p. cm.
  Includes bibliographical references and index.
  ISBN 978-0-7603-2870-5 (hb w/ jkt.)
  1. Historic buildings—Virginia—Pictorial works. 2. Historic buildings—Virginia. 3. Dwellings—Virginia—Pictorial works. 4. Dwellings—Virginia. 5. Historic gardens—Virginia—Pictorial works. 6. Historic gardens—Virginia. 7. Virginia—History, Local—Pictorial works. 8. Virginia—History, Local. 9. Virginia—Biography. I. Blackley, Chuck. II. Title.
  F227.B575 2009
  975.5—dc22

                              2008024209

Editor: Josh Leventhal
Designer: Kazuko Collins

Printed in China

CONTENTS

Preface   6

Introduction   8

Part I: The Tidewater
Adam Thoroughgood House   16
Lee Hall Mansion   20
Smith's Fort Plantation   22
Bacon's Castle   24
Berkeley Plantation   28
Shirley Plantation   34
Appomattox Manor   38

**Part II: Northern Virginia and the
Northern Neck**
Stratford Hall Plantation   40
Mary Washington House   44
Kenmore   46
Gunston Hall   50
Woodlawn Plantation   54
Mount Vernon   58
Carlyle House   64
Oatlands Plantation   68

Part III: Capital Region and Central Virginia
Virginia's Executive Mansion   73
The John Marshall House   76
Maymont   80
Scotchtown   84
Montpelier   86
Monticello   90
Ash Lawn–Highland   96
Point of Honor   100
Poplar Forest   102
Prestwould Plantation   104

Part IV: West of the Blue Ridge
Long Branch   106
Abram's Delight   110
Glen Burnie   112
Belle Grove Plantation   116
The Woodrow Wilson Birthplace   120
Smithfield Plantation   122

Glossary of Terms   124
Bibliography   126
Index   128

ABOVE: *Ornate fireplace mantel, a gift to George Washington from friend and admirer Samuel Vaughan, in the large dining room at Mount Vernon.*

Preface

Established more than four hundred years ago and holding the distinction of being the Birthplace of the Nation, the Commonwealth of Virginia has more than its fair share of historic homes. These homes survive as enduring examples of architectural styles and preferences that were prevalent during Virginia's early years. More importantly, they tell us fascinating stories of the people who lived in them. Volumes have been written about great American figures such as Thomas Jefferson and George Washington. But by visiting their homes, we learn intimate details about their lifestyles that help us to know them not only as brilliant statesmen but also as husbands, fathers, grandfathers, and friends.

It was impossible to include all of the Commonwealth's historic homes in *Virginia's Historic Homes and Gardens*. We have tried to include a variety from across the state, both urban and rural, simple and extravagant, all of which are open to the public, and most of which are National and State Historic Landmarks. Chosen on the basis of their architectural and/or historical significance, they were the houses of many of Virginia's most prominent citizens of the seventeenth, eighteenth, and nineteenth centuries. Seven were homes or birthplaces of six of Virginia's eight U.S. presidents.

We should all be profoundly grateful to the individuals, groups, cities, and others who had the foresight to save and preserve these treasured homes for the enjoyment and enlightenment of future generations. The Mount Vernon Ladies' Association led the way in 1853 with the establishment of a nonprofit foundation for the purpose of raising the funds needed to save and restore Mount Vernon. Since then, other groups of concerned citizens have done the same to rescue endangered properties and open them to the public as historic house museums. Many are included in this book. Several of the book's homes have been preserved through the generosity and thoughtfulness of their last private owners. Some of these owners willed or donated their homes to established preservation organizations or to other private or public entities, which oversee their maintenance and operation. Others established and endowed private foundations to manage and maintain the properties after their deaths.

The National Trust for Historic Preservation (www.preservationnation.org) has helped to preserve America's historic places since it was founded in 1949. Four of its five Virginia properties appear in this book, including its very first trust-administered site, Woodlawn. APVA Preservation Virginia (www.apva.org), established in 1889, is the oldest statewide historic preservation organization in the nation. It has acquired and preserved numerous structures and sites across the state, including six homes that are included in this book. It cannot be stressed enough how valuable the work of both of these nonprofit organizations is in helping to preserve and restore historic properties and to interpret them for the public. Both rely on the generosity of members and volunteers to fulfill their mission.

We also acknowledge the extraordinary work of the Garden Club of Virginia, which provided garden restorations or re-creations for many of this book's properties. Since 1929, proceeds from their annual Historic Garden Week have been used to fund their garden restoration projects, the first of which was Kenmore in Fredericksburg.

It should also be pointed out that most of these houses remain works in progress to some degree. In ongoing research and restoration studies, new discoveries are made that lead to changes and further restorations as funds become available. For example, since we began the photography for this book, several houses have already made changes in paint or wall coverings in certain rooms. Because three of the houses had just completed or were in the middle of restoration projects when we photographed, their rooms held no furnishings. Kenmore, for instance, had just finished a major restoration that, among other things, restored its elaborate ceiling plasterwork. James Madison's Montpelier was in the last stages of a multiyear restoration that returned the home to its Madison-era appearance. Only a few rooms were complete enough for us to photograph. Restoration at Thomas Jefferson's Poplar Forest is ongoing and will be completed in stages over a number of years. We ask that you be mindful as you view these images that certain details may look different when you visit the homes. This is yet another reason that it's worthwhile to revisit them multiple times over the years to appreciate the fruit of the ongoing research at each home.

Working on *Virginia's Historic Homes and Gardens* was a pleasure. The properties were a joy to visit and photograph. We are grateful to the owners, directors, managers, curators, public-relations staffs, docents, gardeners, and others who so graciously and eagerly assisted us with the project by providing helpful research materials, access to the properties, and hours of their valuable time. We were greatly impressed by their obvious pride and affection for these historic homes and gardens.

ABOVE: *The west front facade of George Washington's Mount Vernon is viewed across the expansive bowling green. Several of the large trees that border the green today were planted by Washington when he developed the area in 1785.*

Introduction

The Settling of Virginia

On May 14, 1607, three small English ships—the *Susan Constant*, the *Godspeed*, and the *Discovery*—put ashore on a small, marshy peninsula on the James River in Virginia, part of the mysterious New World. The fleet carried an assemblage of would-be colonists who were ready and anxious to start a new life in this land of opportunity. They were backed by the Virginia Company, a business venture formed by a group of Londoners whose goals were to stake England's claim on the land before the Spanish could beat them to it and then to exploit all of its presumed riches.

Many of the 104 men on board were the younger sons of English gentry. In seventeenth-century England, where a family's firstborn son inherited everything, these men had little hope for a prosperous future at home. The prospect of making their fortunes in a new land was irresistible. The rest of the colonists were primarily working-class artisans hoping to find opportunities not available to them in England.

The colonists named their new home Jamestown, after King James I, and set about establishing what would be the first permanent English settlement in the New World. But it nearly failed—more than once. Most of the colonists were quite inept at dealing with life in the wilderness. Although fish and game abounded, they nearly starved because few knew how to fish or hunt. They were plagued by disease, hostile natives, poor leadership, and a surplus of those soft sons of English gentry who were not willing to do their share of the work. Eight months later, when ships carrying supplies and one hundred new settlers arrived, they found just thirty-eight survivors.

Only the leadership of John Smith, who was elected president of the local council in September 1608, saved the fledgling settlement. He organized and disciplined the colonists, declaring, "He who does not work will not eat." Jamestown survived and even grew over the next year as two more groups of settlers arrived, including women and children. But an accident sent Smith back to England. Then a summer drought produced a scant harvest, leaving hundreds of colonists with meager food supplies to face the brutal winter of 1609–10. This winter became known as the Starving Time. By spring, only sixty settlers remained. The hopeless colonists decided to abandon Jamestown, but as they were sailing away, they were intercepted by supply ships and the new governor, Lord De La Warr. Jamestown would live to see another day.

During the following years, hardships were plentiful, but the colonists persevered. One of them, John Rolfe, rose to the occasion and became instrumental in ensuring the colony's survival. First, by marrying chief Powhatan's daughter, Pocahontas, in 1614, he created a temporary climate of cooperation with the Native Americans. Next, he planted the first crop of West Indian tobacco, which turned out to be the economic saving grace of the colony.

The Virginia Company's profits never met expectations, and England's support of the company waned over the years. Finally, in 1624, after an upsurge in Indian attacks and disease caused a sharp population decline, England revoked the Virginia Company's charter, and Virginia became a royal colony.

By 1630, some five thousand settlers were living in Virginia, concentrated along the navigable rivers in the lower Tidewater, mainly the James and York. Tobacco was the mainstay of the economy. Large land tracts called "hundreds" had been granted to individuals and groups who established tobacco plantations. To attract workers for these labor-intensive plantations and for the other jobs required to develop and settle the colony, the Crown used what Virginia had plenty of: land. Under the headrights system, individuals who paid the transportation costs of immigrants to Virginia received 50 acres for each immigrant. Many new settlers came as indentured servants, hoping to acquire land and start farms of their own after completing their terms of service. Virginia planters also received 50 acres for each slave that they imported to work on their plantations.

ABOVE: *A view of the rear or south side of Thomas Jefferson's octagonal retreat home at Poplar Forest reveals classical details such as the roof balustrade with Chinese rail and the pediment-roofed portico with fanlight, Tuscan columns, and arched openings below.*

These policies led to the accumulation of vast landholdings by an elite group of early colonists, and by the mid-seventeenth century, what would become known as the Virginia aristocracy began to form. It included names such as Byrd, Carter, Washington, Harrison, Randolph, and Lee. Joining them were wealthy English gentry who, as Cavaliers (supporters of the king), had fled to Virginia during the English Civil War (1642–1646). For over a century, these prominent families, who increased their wealth and connections through intermarriages with other important families (and with members of their own extended families), would rule the colony, serving in the House of Burgesses and holding important offices.

Settlement into the mid-1600s continued along the rivers of the Tidewater, westward to the Fall Line, the zone where the soft soil of the coastal plain meets the hard rock of the central plain. There

protruding rocks and rough whitewater made the rivers upstream unnavigable. Naturally, the first settlers chose to establish their farms east of the Fall Line, where they had easy access to oceangoing vessels bound for Europe. But since tobacco rapidly depletes the soil, there was a constant need for more land to cultivate. Consequently, as the Tidewater filled up, planters and new settlers were forced to look elsewhere in their pursuit of land. By the middle of the seventeenth century, they were settling north, along the Chesapeake Bay and into the Northern Neck, along the Potomac River. And by the early eighteenth century, settlement was advancing westward into the colony's Piedmont. Piedmont farmers transported their crops by wagon or small boat to port towns that had developed on the rivers below the Fall Line. There the crops were loaded onto ships for export.

Also by the early eighteenth century, interest was growing in the land west of the Blue Ridge Mountains. The Crown wanted to expand the colony quickly, since it received no income from unsettled lands. Settlement of the frontier was also desirable as a buffer against the Indians and, since the French were already in control of lands just to the west, as a means of firmly establishing Britain's claim on the territory. In 1716, Governor Alexander Spotswood led a group of men, dubbed the Knights of the Golden Horseshoe, on a western real-estate speculation expedition. They crossed over the mountains through Swift Run Gap into the beautiful Shenandoah Valley. Though they returned with glowing reports of the fertile valley they found, the news did not initially attract easterners, since the mountains were still considered a formidable barrier to settlement. However, between 1729 and 1745, the Crown issued large land grants to individuals and groups who vowed to increase settlement west of the mountains.

FACING PAGE: In the formal dining room at Prestwould in Clarksville, diners were cooled by a fan that was mounted on the ceiling and manually operated by a servant who pulled the attached rope at the side of the room. Early-1800s French scenic wallpaper adorns the far wall.

Although the western frontier represented new opportunities for certain Tidewater families, most of its settlers did not come from the east. Beginning in the late 1600s, German and Scotch-Irish immigrants flocked to Pennsylvania seeking religious freedom. By the late 1720s, much of Pennsylvania's farmland had been claimed. New settlers, many of them Mennonite and Quaker farmers, began moving southwest along the Great Wagon Road (now Route 11), through Maryland, and into the Shenandoah Valley and beyond. The cultural and social makeup of western Virginia was therefore quite different from that east of the mountains. Western Virginia was composed primarily of Quakers, Mennonites, and Presbyterians living on mostly smaller plantations and farms, growing grains and corn, with fewer slaves. In the mainly Anglican Piedmont and Tidewater, there were more large farms and plantations and a much greater slave population.

Virginia's Architecture

Initially, the first Jamestown colonists lived in tents and huts, but eventually they began constructing small clapboard houses. Intended to be temporary, for the most part they were built on wooden earth-fast posts with dirt or raised board floors, although some had wooden block or brick foundations and brick floors and chimneys. These dwellings were economical and quick to construct.

As the century progressed and more colonists arrived and settled throughout the Tidewater, they built post-hole dwellings that resembled the houses of their English homelands. Those houses commonly had sharp-pitched roofs, casement windows, and tall end chimneys, and featured a hall-and-parlor plan that included two rooms—a hall and a chamber or parlor. A ladder or primitive stairway accessed a loft that was used for storage or as sleeping quarters for children. Landscaping was simple, and gardens were purely utilitarian. Fenced to keep out animals, gardens were planted with foodstuffs and plants used for dyes, scents, and medicines.

Even most of the first generation of the Virginia aristocracy had no interest in building elaborate houses. Their main objective was to acquire land and amass wealth, and most lived in modest wooden houses. Some of the gentry built brick versions of the post-hole houses with the hall-and-parlor plan, while others built homes of the same plan but with a permanent foundation (such as the Adam Thoroughgood house in Virginia Beach). This style became more sophisticated as time went on, with classical elements such as carved cornices and raised paneling being added. One notable exception to the small, unassuming early gentry houses was Arthur Allen's (Bacon's Castle) impressive three-story brick home—a most unusual dwelling for its time.

In 1699, Virginia's capital was moved from Jamestown to Middle Plantation (later renamed Williamsburg). With the building of the College of William and Mary, the Capitol building, and the Governor's Palace in the early 1700s, a new standard of architecture was introduced in Virginia.

FACING PAGE: *"Light Horse Harry" Lee and his second wife, Ann Hill Carter Lee, were residing at Stratford Hall when Ann gave birth to their son, Robert E. Lee, on January 19, 1807, in the master chamber of the home.*

Those buildings were much larger and grander than anything previously seen in the colonies. The beautiful Governor's Palace was a masterpiece of the English Renaissance architecture popular at the time.

At that same time, later generations of Virginia's aristocracy were coming into their own. They were well educated, culturally refined, and fabulously wealthy, having inherited the land and fortunes of their fathers. Impressed by the beautiful architecture they saw in Williamsburg and the elegant country estates they encountered in their travels or schooling in England, they were anxious to emulate the lavish lifestyles of the English gentry, of which they considered themselves a part. A grand plantation house, built in the English Georgian architectural style, became the ultimate symbol of wealth and social status. It was a style that emphasized balance and symmetry and incorporated classical architectural elements from Rome and Greece. Many stately Georgian mansions, such as Shirley, appeared on Virginia plantations from the early 1700s through the end of the colonial period.

Built primarily of brick, typical houses were two or three stories with the interiors symmetrically arranged with four rooms on each floor. Deviations from the English Georgian style were adapted to deal with the differences in Virginia's available building materials and its climate. Central halls and cross passages, for instance, came about because of the need for cross-ventilation in the warm Virginia climate. These well-lit and breeze-cooled passages became summer living and dining spaces, and many of them, such as that at Berkeley, doubled as ballrooms. Skilled English artisans, many of whom were indentured servants, created the finely carved woodwork and plasterwork found at homes like Kenmore or Gunston Hall, the designs for which came from English pattern books.

The manor house was the nucleus of the plantation, which was usually a complete, self-sufficient community. Surrounding the house were dependencies that included detached kitchens, laundries, dairies, smokehouses, plantation offices, and servants' quarters. Farther away from the house were the barns, stables, mills, and workshops. Food, clothing, and shelter for the families as well as the slaves and servants were all grown or manufactured on the plantation.

The landscaping and gardens of these wealthy planters reflected the same sophistication as

their houses, as they again looked to England for stylistic ideas. They planned the landscaping to include the whole picture—the house, the surrounding grounds, views of the river—and incorporated elements from art and literature. Gardens, both kitchen and pleasure, were often planted in grids with beds separated by walkways or in parterres (beds arranged in patterns) and surrounded by walls or fences. Boxwoods were used as accents, as borders, or in parterres.

West of the Blue Ridge, there were few large, elaborate houses built during the colonial period. Most of the first settlers built small frame houses or log cabins. Eventually, the more affluent German and Scotch-Irish settlers built larger homes, which, though still mainly Georgian in design, incorporated building methods and influences from their homelands. Many were constructed of sturdy limestone, which was plentiful in the Shenandoah Valley. And at Smithfield Plantation, in the stark wilderness of southwest Virginia, early settler William Preston built a fine plantation-style frame home that included many classical features.

The years following the American Revolution brought many changes to Virginia, including architectural ones. Georgian architecture began to yield to a new style known as Federal. Popular between 1780 and 1830, the Federal style became associated with the new American republic and its ideals, although its inspiration came from the work of two Scottish architect brothers, Robert and James Adams. Also known as the "Adamesque" or Adam style, as seen in homes such as Woodlawn, it modified the Georgian design by adding more decorative neoclassical features, such as oval, elliptical, and Palladian windows, roof balustrades, fanlights over the door, curved staircases, and decorative swags and garlands. Moldings, mantels, and cornices were more ornate.

While Georgian houses were rectilinear, Federal-style dwellings featured more curved lines.

Thomas Jefferson, considered to be the first great American-born architect, had a style so distinct it was given its own name: Jeffersonian architecture. Jefferson saw the architecture of ancient Greece as the perfect style to represent the new American republic and advocated its use for government buildings. Using as his "bible" the works of sixteenth-century Italian architect Andrea Palladio, Jefferson designed such public buildings as the Virginia State Capitol (modeled after the Maison Carrée, a Roman temple in Nîmes, France) and the Rotunda at the University of Virginia. His domestic architecture, such as his own Monticello and Poplar Forest, featured the same neoclassical elements, including porticoes with tall columns, domes, and rooms of varying geometric shapes. Jefferson also designed or provided advice on houses for friends, and his influence is seen in numerous homes and buildings throughout the state.

The Georgian, Federal, and Jeffersonian styles or blended variations of them dominated Virginia architecture until the mid-nineteenth century. By that time, Virginia's economy, which had been built largely on tobacco, was stagnating. With the land worn out from overproduction, few new plantation houses were built during the antebellum years. For those that were, such as Lee-Hall Mansion, the Italianate style was a popular design choice. Virginia has few examples of the Greek Revival style that was so popular in the Deep South between 1820 and 1850. George Carter, who had started his mansion at Oatlands in 1804 in the Federal style, altered it in the 1820s to reflect the Greek Revival style.

The Civil War wreaked havoc throughout Virginia. Many of its plantation houses were destroyed. Others served as military headquarters and hospitals. Damaged by cannon fire, marred by soldiers' graffiti, and stained by their blood, many houses came out of the war standing but severely damaged. With their owners left heavily in debt and without a slave work force, most of the large, working plantations ceased to exist.

In the years following the war, Virginia was an economic wasteland, and few grand homes were built. But by the mid-1870s, the Commonwealth was recovering, and new fortunes were being made. During the latter part of the century, some elaborate new houses were being built in the fanciful Victorian styles, such as Queen Anne and Romanesque, an excellent example of which is Richmond's Maymont House. The landscaping and gardens of these estates were as fanciful as the houses themselves. Eclectic in style, they encompassed many different themes, reflecting English, Japanese, and Italian designs in their selection and placement of plantings, statuary, and water features. No expense was spared when it came to creating these fabulous botanical masterpieces.

FACING PAGE, TOP: *The pretty pink flowers of purple loosestrife and the yellow flowers of tickseed create an explosion of color in the perennial garden at Glen Burnie in Winchester.*

FACING PAGE, BOTTOM: *Thomas Jefferson located his magnificent Roman neoclassical mansion at the top of a 987-foot-high mountain on his 5,000-acre plantation in Albemarle County and called his estate Monticello, Italian for "little mountain."*

Part I

THE TIDEWATER

Adam Thoroughgood House

1636 Parish Road
Virginia Beach, VA 23455

The Adam Thoroughgood House, one of the oldest brick dwellings constructed in Virginia, now stands on just under 7 acres in the middle of a modern Virginia Beach housing development. While the exact date of construction is not known, its architecture indicates it was built in the late seventeenth or early eighteenth century. The Department of Museums of the City of Virginia Beach, which owns and manages the historic house, uses the approximate date of 1719.

Adam Thoroughgood came to Virginia from England in 1621 as an indentured servant, but when he died less than twenty years later, he was one of the largest landowners in the colony's southeastern region. After serving out his three-year indentureship, he returned to England in 1624 and married Sarah Offley, the daughter of a wealthy merchant. Together they returned to Virginia in 1628 and made their home in Kecoughton (now Hampton). Thoroughgood recruited and paid the passage for 105 persons to come to Virginia, taking advantage of the headrights system, which rewarded him with 50 acres of land for each new settler he brought over.

In 1636, Thoroughgood received his "Grand Patent" of 5,350 acres lying along the Lynnhaven River in what was then Lower Norfolk County. He and Sarah settled there, becoming the area's founding colonists. It was the largest land patent in the colony at that time, ensuring Thoroughgood a position of prominence in Virginia society. Committed to public service, he was a member of the House of Burgesses and was appointed to the Governor's Royal Council, a small group of men who helped determine policy in the colony. He was also a captain in the militia, a county justice, and a vestryman. He achieved all of this by 1640, the year he died at the age of thirty-six.

A descendant, most likely a grandson, built the house that is known today as the Adam Thoroughgood House on a section of the original 5,350 acres, and it remained in the Thoroughgood family until the 1860s. After that, it changed hands many times, enduring many changes along the way, before being acquired by the Thoroughgood Foundation, which undertook a complete restoration in 1957. The City of Norfolk owned the house from 1961 until 2003, when it was acquired by the City of Virginia Beach.

The one-and-a-half-story brick house has a steep gabled roof and massive end chimneys—one projecting, the other set inside the wall. The west wall brickwork is laid in Flemish bond, while the other three sides are laid in English bond.

Inside, the house has a central hall plan with one room on each side of a center hall or passage, and a stairway rises to a second floor with two rooms. It appears that the house may have first originated as a hall-and-parlor-style home, with just one room and the hall downstairs and a narrow steep stair that accessed an upstairs loft. Most of the fine paneling and wainscoting in the north parlor and passage are original to the early eighteenth century. The south parlor (which would also have been used for cooking and dining) has been restored to interpret the late seventeenth century, with an

open beam ceiling typical of that period. Other ceilings on the first floor are plastered. In one area, the original plaster, which was made of oyster shells and goat hair, can still be seen.

Outside, crepe myrtles, graceful magnolias, and pecan trees surround the old house, which is open for tours Tuesday through Sunday. An enchanting seventeenth-century pleasure garden, designed by Alden Hopkins, was donated by the Garden Club of Virginia in 1958–59 and 1990. It includes two large plots on each side of a central walkway, with topiary shrubs, flowers, and espaliered fruit trees. Two large arbors are located at the outer boundaries. In June, an explosion of daylilies makes the grounds especially beautiful.

TOP: *Constructed in about 1719, the English-style Adam Thoroughgood House is one of Virginia's earliest permanent brick dwellings. Its distinctive massive end chimneys are typical of the period. The charming, re-created seventeenth-century English "pleasure garden" was designed by the Garden Club of Virginia and is maintained by the Virginia Beach Master Gardeners.*

ABOVE: *From the south parlor, the garden of the Adam Thoroughgood House is seen through reproduction mullioned casement windows. The windows were popular during the late seventeenth and early eighteenth centuries.*

ABOVE LEFT: *The beautiful dark wood paneling and wainscoting in the north parlor were added during an early eighteenth-century remodeling.*

ABOVE RIGHT: *It is believed that the Thoroughgood House originally had a hall-and-parlor plan with a narrow, steep staircase. During an early-eighteenth-century remodeling, it was transformed into the current central-hall plan and given its striking Georgian stairway.*

FACING PAGE, TOP: *The south parlor is restored to the late-seventeenth-century period, with an open-beam ceiling made of yellow heart pine. This was a multifunctional room, used for cooking, eating, reading, and sleeping.*

FACING PAGE, BOTTOM: *Originally, the second-floor loft contained two unheated rooms used for storage and possibly sleeping. Later, fireplaces were added, and this room became the master bedchamber. A second upstairs room most likely was used as the children's sleeping quarters and for storage. The furnishings of this era were comfortable but plain.*

Lee Hall Mansion

163 YORKTOWN ROAD
NEWPORT NEWS, VA 23603

In 1859, wealthy Tidewater planter Richard Decauter Lee moved his family into the handsome new manor house he had built on his large Lower Peninsula plantation. Unfortunately, after living there for just three years, the family was forced to flee from their beautiful home when the area became an early battleground of the Civil War.

In the spring of 1862, Confederate Major General John B. Magruder and General Joseph E. Johnston were in charge of defending the peninsula from the advancing Union army, which was led by Major General George B. McClellan. Because Lee Hall was built on high ground with a view of the surrounding countryside, the generals commandeered the mansion as their Confederate headquarters between April and May of that year and, from there, directed the defense of the peninsula from McClellan's army.

After delaying the Union advance for three weeks, the Confederate army was ordered to retreat on May 3, which they did after fighting a small skirmish with Union cavalry on the property. The Union remained in control of the peninsula until the end of the war.

The Lee family remained in the mansion during part of the campaign but soon fled. They eventually returned to Lee Hall and lived there until 1871. After that, the property passed through many owners before being purchased in 1996 by the City of Newport News. A meticulous restoration followed, which returned the house to its antebellum appearance. Now the city's Department of Parks and Recreation operates it as a historic house museum that documents the 1862 Peninsula Campaign.

Lee Hall Mansion is the last remaining large antebellum plantation house on the Lower Peninsula. The elegant brick two-story mansion, with a full basement, combines many architectural styles, including Georgian and Greek Revival. The primary style, however, is Italianate, which was one of the most popular in America at the time the house was built.

The Italianate style is seen in the mansion's low-hipped roof with wide, overhanging eaves that are supported by a bracketed cornice. Inside, the style is identified in the three original plaster ceiling medallions. The symmetrical floor plan, however, is Georgian, with its classic four-over-four room design.

On the first floor, two rooms lie on either side of a long central hall, the unique feature for which Lee Hall is named. Most antebellum houses did not have hallways, since they were considered to be impractical and a waste of space. Consequently, formal halls were only found in the homes of the wealthy. At Lee Hall, the hall's 12-foot ceiling is decorated with an original plaster rosette depicting a sunflower and acanthus-leaf motif. A hand-painted floorcloth runs the length of the hall. The grand staircase, which is original, leads upstairs to four bedrooms.

To the right of the hall is a formal ladies' parlor, which features another original plaster ceiling rosette. A pair of original pocket doors open into an adjoining gentlemen's parlor. Major General Magruder used the gentlemen's parlor as his headquarters, and the room is interpreted accordingly, with tables spread with maps and Confederate items. Across the hall from the rear parlor is the music room with its grand pianoforte. As in the parlors, a set of pocket doors joins the music room to a large, formal, neoclassical dining room. Upstairs, two of the four rooms have been restored and are interpreted as the master bedroom and a girl's bedroom. All of the restored rooms have been decorated with stylish period furniture, wallpapers, floor coverings, and window treatments. In the basement of the house, a gallery documents the 1862 Peninsula Campaign.

Lee Hall is open for tours Wednesday through Monday from April through December and Thursday through Monday from January through March.

ABOVE: *In 1859, just two years before the start of the Civil War, Richard Decauter Lee built his elegant mansion, Lee Hall, in the picturesque Italianate style. When Virginia's Lower Peninsula became one of the first battlegrounds of the war in 1862, Lee, his wife, Martha, and their three children were forced to vacate their home.*

RIGHT: *When the Confederate army commandeered Lee Hall during the 1862 Peninsula Campaign, Major General John B. Magruder used the gentlemen's parlor as his headquarters. Located off of the central hall, the room connects to the adjoining ladies' parlor through a set of wide pocket doors. The restored house is decorated with exquisite period furnishings, including richly colored wall and floor coverings.*

Smith's Fort Plantation

217 SMITH FORT LANE
SURRY, VA 23883

In 1609, just two years after the founding of Jamestown, Captain John Smith and other Jamestown settlers built an earth fort on a bluff above Gray's Creek in Surry County. The fort, which was located directly across the James River from Jamestown, provided the settlers with a retreat in the event of an attack by hostile natives or by the Spanish. From that point on, the site was known as Smith's Fort.

Five years later, John Rolfe married Pocahontas, the daughter of the powerful Indian chief Powhatan. The chief presented this entire neck of land, which encompassed some 2,000 acres, to Rolfe as a dower gift. The Rolfes' son, Thomas, who was born and raised in England, inherited the land from his father, and in 1635 he came to Virginia to claim it.

By the mid-1700s, 590 acres of this land had been acquired by Nicholas Faulcon. Between 1761 and 1765, Faulcon built a house on the plantation for his son, Jacob, who lived there with his wife, Anne, and their five children. Jacob served as an officer in the Revolutionary War and then became the clerk of Surry County, a position he held from 1781 until 1801.

TOP: *Situated on the south side of the James River directly across from Jamestown, Smith's Fort Plantation was named for the earthen fort built on the property by Captain John Smith and other Jamestown settlers in 1609. The current mid-Georgian-style manor house was built around 1765 by Nicholas Faulcon for his son, Jacob.*

The Faulcon family owned the property until 1835. After that, it had many owners before the Colonial Williamsburg Foundation purchased the property in 1928. Then, in 1933, the Association for the Preservation of Virginia Antiquities (now APVA Preservation Virginia) acquired Smith's Fort from the Colonial Williamsburg Foundation. It was opened to the public in 1935.

The fully restored dwelling is an excellent example of mid-Georgian-style architecture. The handsome one-and-a-half-story house with a full basement is built of brick laid in Flemish bond. It has a gabled roof with three dormer windows on each side.

The home's interior retains most of the original pine woodwork, including floors, doors, and cupboards. Two rooms on the first floor, a living room or parlor and a master bedchamber, lie to either side of an entry hall. Upstairs there are two additional bedchambers. The parlor is especially lovely, with its carved chimney piece, fluted pilasters, paneling, and cornice. On either side of the fireplace are elegant arched cupboards with butterfly shelves, known as beaufats. The rooms are furnished with a fine collection of seventeenth- and eighteenth-century British and American antiques.

The Garden Club of Virginia completed a restoration of the grounds, which now include 27 acres, in 1937. At the back of the house, the club designed and planted a boxwood garden and small herb and flower gardens with seventeenth- and eighteenth-century plantings. Magnolia trees were planted in the front, and tulip poplars were planted along the entrance drive.

While at the property, visitors can follow a footpath through the woods that leads to the site of John Smith's original 1609 retreat fort. The now barely visible earthwork is the oldest manmade, aboveground English structure in Virginia.

Smith's Fort Plantation is open for tours Tuesday through Sunday from April through October and on weekends only in March and November.

ABOVE: *The parlor at Smith's Fort boasts exceptionally fine woodwork, with raised paneling and intricately carved cornice, chimney piece, and fluted pilasters. The built-in cupboards that flank the fireplace are known as beaufats. Most of the pine woodwork in the house is original.*

Bacon's Castle

465 BACON'S CASTLE TRAIL
SURRY, VA 23883

In 1665, Surry County planter and merchant Arthur Allen, one of the wealthiest men in the colony, constructed a fine brick Jacobean house on his 700-acre plantation. Jacobean, a seventeenth-century English architectural style noted for its elaborate features, was rarely seen in the colonies due to the high construction costs involved.

As originally constructed, the three-story house with a full English cellar was built in a cruciform shape. The first floor contained two rooms—the hall, which was the main public space, and a chamber. The second story held two additional chambers. (As was typical in colonial-era dwellings, most rooms of the house, including chambers, were multipurpose spaces.) On the third floor, three small rooms known as garrets provided storage space and additional sleeping quarters. The cellar housed a kitchen, service rooms, and storage space.

When Allen died in 1669, the property passed to his son, Arthur Allen II, known as Major Allen. In 1676, Nathaniel Bacon led a rebellion against the British Crown, which Allen, who served as justice of the peace, opposed. For their own safety, Allen's family temporarily left Surry County during the unrest. While they were gone, seventy of Bacon's followers seized and occupied the home for nearly four months. After Bacon died, effectively ending the rebellion, the rebels left the property. Allen's family returned to their home, which was thereafter known as Bacon's Castle.

Arthur Allen III inherited the property when Major Allen died in 1710. He and his wife, Elizabeth, made numerous changes to the house in the early 1700s, including the addition of a central passage that divided the hall from the chamber and the installation of elaborate raised paneling in both rooms.

Ownership of Bacon's Castle passed out of the Allen family in 1843. The John Hankins family then owned it until 1872. In 1854, Hankins added a large neoclassical wing, which was connected to the old section by a two-story passage called a hyphen. The home's last private owners, the Warren family, held it from 1880 until 1973. At that time, APVA Preservation Virginia purchased the house and 40 acres from the estate of Walker Warren and initiated a research and restoration effort. The property was opened to the public in 1983.

The original 1665 section of Bacon's Castle is the oldest brick house in Virginia and stands as a rare and magnificent example of Jacobean domestic architecture with its curved Flemish gables and massive triple-stacked chimneys. The interior reveals other significant architectural details like the carved compass roses that decorate the intersections of many of its ceiling beams and the central, rear stair tower that runs the full height of the dwelling.

The APVA did not try to restore the house to a single time period. Except for the removal of some modern additions, the dwelling's alterations over the years were preserved. Care was taken to salvage and authentically repair as much of the original woodwork as possible. On the upper floors, many of the early and original massive hand-hewn beams can still be seen. The hall is interpreted to the mid-1700s, with furnishings based on an Allen inventory from 1755. An upstairs bedchamber appears as it may have looked in the late seventeenth century, with furnishings based on an inventory taken when Major Allen died in 1710.

In the 1980s, the Garden Club of Virginia sponsored a restoration of the gardens that began with archaeological excavations. Those excavations revealed the remains of outbuildings, plus Bacon's Castle's nineteenth-, eighteenth-, and seventeenth-century gardens. The seventeenth-century garden is one of the earliest and most complete found in North America—an incredible discovery. Based on their findings, the Garden Club re-created the circa-1680 garden at Bacon's Castle. The football-field-sized garden is laid out in a rectangular grid divided into six planting beds, which are separated by white sand walkways. It contains a large variety of late seventeenth-century heirloom vegetables, herbs, and flowers, such as larkspur, hollyhocks, snapdragons, and columbine.

Bacon's Castle is open Tuesday through Sunday from April through October and weekends only in March and November.

ABOVE: *Bacon's Castle, with its huge triple-stacked chimneys and curved Flemish gables, looms behind the colorful spring blossoms of the home's seventeenth-century garden.*

FACING PAGE: *The original portion of Bacon's Castle, Arthur Allen's Surry County plantation home, was built in 1665, making it the oldest brick dwelling in Virginia. The impressive Jacobean-style structure, standing three stories tall above a full basement, was an anomaly for its time and place. The Greek Revival addition on the right was built in 1854.*

ABOVE: *Bacon's Castle holds the best-preserved and documented seventeenth-century garden in the nation. The huge garden consists of six rectangular sections separated by white-sand walkways. A border bed lies outside the outer walkway. The garden contains numerous varieties of flowers, vegetables, fruits, and herbs that would have been found in a late-seventeenth-century garden.*

RIGHT: *One of the many notable architectural features of Bacon's Castle is its central stair tower. The winding staircase runs the full height of the house. Looking down from the upper floors proves to be a dizzying experience.*

FACING PAGE, TOP: *The hall at Bacon's Castle, which was the main public space in the house, was used for eating, socializing, and entertaining. This is one of the rooms that has a carved compass rose at the intersection of its ceiling beams. Arthur Allen III and his wife, Elizabeth, installed the raised paneling in the early 1700s.*

ABOVE: *This second-floor bedchamber appears today as it may have looked in the late seventeenth century, with furnishings based on an inventory that was taken after Major Allen died in 1710. In addition to sleeping, this multifunctional room was also used as a less formal area for working, eating, and socializing.*

Berkeley Plantation

12602 HARRISON LANDING ROAD
CHARLES CITY, VA 23030

One of the oldest and most historic of the James River plantations, Berkeley's long history began on December 4, 1619, when thirty-eight Englishmen who called themselves the Berkeley Company arrived on the shores of the James River. They had sailed from England to settle an 8,000-acre land grant, which they named Berkeley Hundred. On that day, they observed the first official Thanksgiving in America when they held a service to thank God for their safe arrival.

That settlement was destroyed by an Indian attack in 1622. In 1691, Benjamin Harrison III purchased Berkeley and established Harrison's Landing, the first commercial shipyard on the James River. In 1721, his son, Benjamin IV, began building a manor house for himself and his bride, Anne Carter, daughter of the powerful tobacco planter Robert "King" Carter. Five years later, the couple moved into their completed mansion. A date stone placed in the brick wall above a side door contains a heart encircled by their initials and the date 1726.

Berkeley's next owner, Benjamin Harrison V, was a signer of the Declaration of Independence and a three-time governor of Virginia. His younger son, William Henry Harrison, became the ninth president of the United States in 1841. Forty-eight years later, William's grandson, another Benjamin Harrison, served as the twenty-third U.S. president.

Berkeley changed hands several times after it left the Harrison family's control in the 1840s. For two months during the Civil War, Union General George McClellan's troops occupied Berkeley. While 140,000 soldiers camped in the fields, McClellan used the home's second floor as his headquarters, the first floor as a hospital, and the basement as a Confederate prison. It was during this time that General Daniel Butterfield, who was with McClellan's forces at Berkeley, composed the army's official bugle call, "Taps." The song was first played here by bugler O. W. Norton. President Abraham Lincoln visited Berkeley twice during McClellan's occupation.

Berkeley sat abandoned for many years after the war. In 1907, John Jamieson of Scotland, a former drummer boy with McClellan's forces at Berkeley, bought the house and 1,400 acres. Jamieson's son, Malcolm, inherited the deteriorating property in 1927. He and his wife, Grace, whom he married in 1933, lovingly restored the house and grounds to their eighteenth-century splendor. They filled the house with magnificent eighteenth-century antiques and opened the grounds, the first floor, and the basement to the public. Still a working plantation, Berkeley remains in the Jamieson family today and is open all year.

The stately, three-story, brick, Georgian mansion, which sits on a lushly landscaped hilltop overlooking the James River, is crowned with what is believed to be the first pediment roof in Virginia. In the house's basement, one can observe the massive timber beams and hand-hewn joists that, along with the solid 3-foot walls, have supported the mansion for nearly three centuries. All the building materials for the house except the brass came from the plantation.

Berkeley has the typical Georgian four-room, center-hall floor plan. The wide, 40-foot-long entry hall was also used as a ballroom, so Benjamin IV did not place the main staircase here lest dancing space be lost. Located to one side of the hall are a formal dining room and a gentleman's room. On the other side are north and south drawing rooms, which are joined by graceful double arches with fluted pilasters. These were added when Benjamin Harrison VI remodeled the house in

1790, with advice from Thomas Jefferson on the plans. Also at that time, the mansion's original pine paneling was removed, the walls were plastered, and the beautiful hand-carved Adam-style cornices and chair moldings were added.

A quarter-mile path that descends from the mansion to the river passes through five terraced gardens that were hand dug by slaves before the Revolutionary War. Berkeley's 10 acres of formal gardens include boxwood parterres, roses, and a ladies' winter garden. Flowering trees such as dogwood, redbud, magnolia, and crape myrtle add to the beauty. Wooded paths also lead to the "Taps" and First Thanksgiving monuments and to the Harrison family graveyard.

TOP: *Berkeley Plantation's stately Georgian manor house, built in 1726, was the home of the prominent Harrison family, whose members included a signer of the Declaration of Independence and Virginia governor, as well as two U.S. presidents. This view of the house is from the carriage entrance. During plantation days, most visitors arrived at the house from the river side, which was considered the front of the house.*

ABOVE: *Berkeley's builder, Benjamin Harrison IV, and his wife, Anne Carter Harrison, placed on the west end of the house this circular date stone, in which they carved their initials, a heart, and the date of the home's completion.*

FACING PAGE, TOP: *A portrait of the ninth president of the United States, William Henry Harrison, who was born at Berkeley in 1773, hangs above the mantel in the formal dining room. Above the sideboard is a portrait of Grace Jamieson, who, together with her husband, Malcolm, restored Berkeley to its former grandeur.*

RIGHT: *The home's entry hall is 40 feet long with doors at each end. The Harrisons frequently used the hall as a ballroom. During the warm summer months, both doors could be opened wide so that guests could be cooled by the refreshing cross breezes.*

BELOW: *Berkeley's north and south drawing rooms are connected by elegant, double-arched doorways. The arches, as well as the Adamesque cornice and chair molding, were part of a remodeling undertaken by Benjamin Harrison VI in 1790, with design guidance provided by Thomas Jefferson. The portrait above the fireplace is of Benjamin Harrison V, signer of the Declaration of Independence and three-time Virginia governor.*

ABOVE: *The gentleman's room was used both as a bedchamber and as the planter's office. By the window, the walnut William and Mary chest, made in 1690, is the oldest piece of furniture at Berkeley.*

LEFT: *Berkeley's 10 acres of formal terraced gardens include flowering trees such as dogwood, redbud, and crape myrtle, as well as boxwood parterres, roses, and a ladies' winter garden.*

FACING PAGE, BOTTOM: *A quarter-mile path leads from the house down to the James River. After purchasing Berkeley Plantation in 1691, Benjamin Harrison III established Harrison's Landing along his more than two miles of waterfront. The busy commercial center grew to include a shipyard and an export tobacco warehouse.*

BELOW: *A shady, tree-lined path leads to monuments that recognize the first Thanksgiving and the composing of "Taps," as well as to the Harrison family graveyard.*

Shirley Plantation

501 SHIRLEY PLANTATION ROAD
CHARLES CITY, VA 23030

Just six years after the 1607 settlement of Jamestown, Sir Thomas West, the third Baron De La Warr, received a royal grant of approximately 4,000 acres of land along the James River. There he established Virginia's first tobacco plantation, naming it West and Sherley Hundred after himself and his wife, Lady Cessalye Sherley, although they never lived on the plantation. When Sir Thomas died in 1618, the land was sold and passed through many hands over the following decades.

In 1638, Edward Hill I established a tobacco farm on 450 acres of the land, and by 1660, he had patented 2,476 acres of the Sherley Hundred property. Three-and-a-half centuries later, that enterprise, which became known as Shirley Plantation, is still owned, managed, and worked by Hill's descendants—making it the oldest family business in America.

The plantation's first dwelling, Hill House, was occupied by three generations of the Hill family. By 1700, Edward Hill III was the master of Shirley. When his only son (Edward IV) died at age sixteen, the inheritance rights to Shirley passed to his daughter, Elizabeth. Elizabeth united two of Virginia's most prominent families when she married John Carter, the eldest son of Robert "King" Carter, the wealthiest man in the colony. From there, the powerful dynasty continued to expand as future generations of Carters married into other distinguished Virginia families, including the Byrds, Harrisons, Randolphs, and Lees.

In 1723, John Carter began building Shirley's current manor house, which was completed in 1738. One of the most beautiful of the colonial plantation homes, Shirley is a magnificent three-story, Georgian-style dwelling with a symmetrical four-room floor plan that is repeated on all three floors. The distinctive house, a 48-foot cube topped by a mansard roof with projecting dormer windows, is of an architectural style similar to that of the Governor's Palace in Williamsburg. The handsome brick mansion overlooks four original brick dependencies, which are arranged symmetrically in a Queen Anne forecourt, typical of English estates.

Located in the entrance hall is one of Shirley's most unique features, a square-rigged "flying" staircase that rises for three stories with no visible means of support. The elegant staircase, with its lustrous black walnut banister, is original to the house and the only one of its kind remaining in America.

The Great House remains remarkably unaltered, with doors and locks and yellow pine floors all original to its early 1700s construction. In 1771, when Charles Carter inherited the house, he added rich interior paneling, beautifully carved woodwork, and pocket shutters. On the exterior, he added two gracious double porticos and crowned the mansion's roof with the large carved pineapple finial, which was a colonial-era symbol of hospitality. As a hub of colonial society, Shirley's hospitality was extended to many prominent Virginians, including George Washington and Thomas Jefferson. Today, the eleventh generation of the Carter family still welcomes guests who come to admire this beautifully preserved example of colonial plantation life.

FACING PAGE: *From the time it was acquired by Edward Hill in 1638, Shirley Plantation has belonged to eleven generations of the Hill and Carter families. The striking Georgian manor house, completed in 1738 by John Carter, overlooks a Queen Anne forecourt with four original dependencies that include a kitchen, laundry, storehouse, and icehouse.*

RIGHT: *With the Great House visible through the trees in the background, springtime finds azaleas in bloom in one of Shirley's landscaped gardens.*

Shirley has survived numerous trials and ordeals throughout its long history, including tragic deaths, fire, the Great Depression, and two wars. During the American Revolution, it served as a supply depot for Lafayette's troops. After the Civil War's nearby Battle of Malvern Hill, Shirley's grounds served as a field hospital for thousands of wounded Union soldiers. The Carter women of Shirley put their Southern allegiances aside and helped to care for the wounded enemy soldiers. Afterward, a grateful General George McClellan issued a Federal Order of Safeguard for Shirley, which protected it for the rest of the war.

Shirley's first floor is open for tours daily, all year. The top floors are still occupied by the Carter family. The entry hall, parlor, dining room, and bedchamber are filled with original family furnishings and silver, and the walls are lined with seventeenth- and eighteenth-century portraits of early Hill-Carter family members.

Also included with admission to the plantation are access to Shirley's scenic grounds and to its original outbuildings, which display exhibits, artifacts, and information panels. A small formal garden features boxwood, perennials, herbs, and a grape arbor. Shirley continues to operate as a working plantation today.

BELOW: *As it drops low over the James River, the late-afternoon sun lights up Shirley's columned portico. The two double porticos at Shirley were added during Charles Carter's 1771 renovations. The massive willow oak tree at the edge of the lawn has anchored that spot for approximately 350 years.*

RIGHT: *One of Shirley's most notable architectural features is its magnificent square-rigged "flying staircase." Though it appears to rise for three floors with no visible means of support, it is actually supported by wrought-iron straps. As the only staircase in the house, it has carried family, guests, and servants daily for close to three centuries.*

BELOW: *In 1793, Anne Hill Carter, the eldest daughter of Charles and Anne Carter, married Henry "Light Horse Harry" Lee in the parlor at Shirley. They would later become parents of future Confederate General Robert E. Lee. The most elaborate room in the house, the parlor features splendid carved Georgian woodwork, including the intricate cornice, overdoor decorations, and fireplace mantel.*

Appomattox Manor

In 1613, Captain Francis Eppes sailed from England to Virginia aboard a ship named the *Hopewell*. By 1635, he had acquired land on the tip of a peninsula overlooking the confluence of the Appomattox and James Rivers. There he established a plantation, known as Appomattox. Remarkably, that property would remain in Eppes' family for nearly 350 years.

Over the years, the little port town of City Point, which had first been established as *Bermuda Cittie* in 1613, grew up around the plantation. During the Civil War's Siege of Petersburg (June 1864 to April 1865), General Ulysses S. Grant made City Point, including Appomattox Plantation and its manor house, the headquarters and supply base for the Union army. Overnight, the tiny village became one of the busiest ports in the world as hundreds of ships arrived, bringing food, clothing, and ammunition. The old town of City Point, annexed by the City of Hopewell in 1923, is now a National Historic District.

Although evidence of a seventeenth-century house was found at Appomattox Plantation, the original section of the current manor house dates from 1763. At that time, Richard Eppes constructed a 20-foot by 50-foot, one-and-a-half-story, white frame house with a cellar. Each floor had a center hall with one room on each side. During the nineteenth century, Dr. Richard Eppes, the great-grandson of the original builder, added east and west wings, which brought the total number of rooms in the house to twenty-three.

Even though Dr. Eppes had 130 slaves on his plantation, which by the mid-1800s included 2,300 acres, he did not favor secession. However, when the Civil War started, Eppes enlisted in the 3rd Virginia Cavalry. In May 1862, his wife and children left the plantation for the safety of Petersburg, and they later fled to her family's home in Pennsylvania. Eppes eventually became a civilian contract surgeon for the Confederate army in Petersburg until the war ended.

When General Grant established the Union headquarters at City Point, he and his staff initially lived in tents on Appomattox Manor's east lawn. Eventually, the tents were replaced by twenty-two small log cabins. United States Quartermaster Rufus Ingalls and his staff used the manor house for offices.

After the war, Dr. Eppes had to buy back the title for his heavily damaged plantation from the federal government before he could make repairs and bring his family home. All structures left behind by the army also had to be purchased from the government before Eppes could remove them.

The Eppes family occupied the house until 1954. After that, various relatives and friends lived there until 1979, when the National Park Service acquired the property and made it a part of the City Point Unit of the Petersburg National Battlefield.

A National Park Visitor Center is located inside the house. The parlor and the library have been restored to their antebellum appearance and are furnished with Eppes family pieces. Future plans call for the restoration of the entire first floor.

The grounds contain plantation outbuildings, wayside exhibits, and a lovely crape myrtle allée. General Grant's two-room log cabin, which was moved to Philadelphia after the Civil War, was purchased by the National Park Service in 1981 and reconstructed on its original site on the plantation's grounds.

ABOVE: *The vibrant blossoms of crape myrtle frame the manor house at Appomattox Plantation, the oldest part of which was built in 1763. The plantation was first settled by the Eppes family in 1635. The site is now part of the City Point Unit of Petersburg National Battlefield. On June 15, 1864, General Ulysses S. Grant established his Union headquarters on the sprawling grounds of the plantation.*

RIGHT: *The library is one of two rooms in the manor house that have been restored to their antebellum appearance and furnished with Eppes family pieces. By the time of the Civil War, Dr. Richard Eppes, the owner of the plantation at that time, was one of the wealthiest men in Virginia.*

Part II

NORTHERN VIRGINIA
&
THE NORTHERN NECK

Stratford Hall Plantation

483 GREAT HOUSE ROAD
STRATFORD, VA 22558

The "Great House" that sits atop high bluffs overlooking the Potomac River on Virginia's Northern Neck is the seat of the Lee family, one of the most distinguished political and military families in Virginia history. Built in the late 1730s by Thomas Lee, the house was the center of a thriving plantation complex. A successful planter, businessman, and land speculator, Thomas was also an important political figure in colonial Virginia, holding such positions as Naval Officer of the Potomac, member of the House of Burgesses, and acting governor of Virginia.

Thomas and Hannah Lee had six children, two of whom, Richard Henry and Francis Lightfoot, were the only brothers to sign the Declaration of Independence. When he died in 1750, Thomas left Stratford to his eldest son, Philip Ludwell Lee. After Philip's death, the house and surrounding property passed to his daughter, Matilda, who married her cousin, Revolutionary War hero Henry "Light Horse Harry" Lee. Three years after Matilda died, her husband, who was left with a life interest in Stratford, married Ann Hill Carter of Shirley Plantation. Ann gave birth to their son, future Confederate General Robert E. Lee, on January 19, 1807, at Stratford Hall. Robert was not yet four when his family moved to Alexandria, but he visited Stratford throughout his childhood and always held a deep fondness for his birthplace.

Stratford remained in the Lee family until the 1820s. It then passed through two other families before the nonprofit Robert E. Lee Memorial Association purchased the mansion, outbuildings, and 1,100 acres in 1929. Their mission was to preserve it in honor of General Lee and the other Lees of Stratford Hall. After a meticulous restoration, it was opened to the public as a museum that interprets the plantation life of the Lee family. It is open for tours daily, year round.

Built in about 1738, Thomas Lee's "Great House" is a very large, two-story, Georgian dwelling built of bricks fired on the plantation. The brick is laid in Flemish bond, with glazing added to the header bricks below the protruding water table for visual appeal. The home's unique H-shaped layout features two large rectangular wings on either side of a center block. Clusters of four huge chimney stacks, bound together by arches, are centered over each wing. The arches enclose balustraded platforms that rise above the mansion's hipped roof. At one time, a promenade platform ran between the two clusters.

The interior arrangement is unusual for colonial dwellings. The raised main floor contains the formal living spaces. The most public room of the house, the Great Hall, makes up the center block. Recognized as an outstanding example of Georgian symmetry, this beautiful room is 29 feet square with a 17-foot-high tray, or coved, ceiling. There are four tall windows, two exterior doors, and two

ABOVE: *Thomas Lee built the imposing H-shaped Georgian Great House on his Stratford Hall Plantation between 1730 and 1738, and Robert E. Lee, future Confederate general, was born in the house in 1807. The large tobacco plantation on the Potomac included a wharf, a warehouse, a gristmill, a ship's store, and numerous workshops.*

LEFT: *The centerpiece of the formal east garden is a center oval that holds an English armillary sphere. Initially restored by the Garden Club of Virginia in the 1930s, the eighteenth-century English-style garden consists of four terraces that descend to a restored eighteenth-century ha-ha wall. Parterres outlined with boxwood are planted with period bulbs, annuals, and perennials. Crape myrtle and other flowering shrubs provide additional color.*

passage doors. Pilasters with ornately carved Corinthian capitals adorn its fully paneled walls. On either side of the Great Hall, wings hold the dining room, parlors, library, nursery, and two bedchambers. The ground level of the house contains the less formal areas, such as storage and service rooms, plus additional bedchambers that were used by the children and visitors.

The formal site plan places the house at the center of a square, with brick dependencies at each corner and a formal garden on either side. Various original and reconstructed buildings occupy the current 1,600-acre site, including the reconstructed eighteenth-century gristmill.

The Garden Club of Virginia restored the east garden in the early 1930s in a typical eighteenth-century English style, and various alterations have been made over the years. The terraced garden, planted with crape myrtles and flowering shrubs, is accessed by oyster-shell paths and enclosed by brick walls. Irregular parterres are outlined with English boxwood and planted with bulbs, annuals, and perennials. An English armillary sphere stands in the center of a central oval.

The west garden holds geometric flower beds, accessed by brick paths, containing period perennials, annuals, bulbs, and roses. Adjacent to the flower garden, vegetable and herb gardens are enclosed by borders of espalier-trained fruit trees.

ABOVE: *The Great Hall at Stratford is considered to be one of the most beautiful rooms in the United States. Occupying the center block of the H-shaped mansion, this 29-foot square room with a high tray ceiling was its most public space, used for socializing, entertaining, and dancing. The portrait above the doorway depicts the home's builder, Thomas Lee.*

RIGHT: *One of Stratford Hall's most prominent architectural features is its two massive chimney clusters, each of which consists of four chimneystacks connected by arches that enclose balustraded platforms.*

FACING PAGE: *The recently renovated west garden is a lovely example of an eighteenth-century flower garden. Period varieties of annuals, perennials, and bulbs fill geometric beds that are separated by brick walkways.*

Mary Washington House

1200 CHARLES STREET
FREDERICKSBURG, VA 22401

George Washington's mother, Mary Ball Washington, was still living at Ferry Farm when she was sixty-four years old. Located across the Rappahannock River from Fredericksburg, Ferry Farm had been her home since her late husband, Augustine, moved the family there in 1738. Augustine died at the age of forty-nine, leaving his thirty-five-year-old widow with five young children. In his will, Augustine left the farm to George, but he left Mary control of it as long as she did not remarry. When George inherited Mount Vernon from his older half-brother, Lawrence, in 1754, he moved to Mount Vernon, while his mother remained at Ferry Farm.

In 1772, Washington decided that his aging mother needed to move from the farm into the town of Fredericksburg to be near her children Betty, Charles, and Samuel. He purchased a small cottage just two blocks from Kenmore, the home that Betty and her husband were building.

The original one-and-a-half-story white frame cottage, which was approximately ten years old when Washington purchased it, consisted of two downstairs rooms with a loft above. He knocked out a wall between the two rooms, making it one large room that was used as a combination bedroom/sitting room. Then he added a two-story addition to the house that included a front hall, a parlor, an upstairs bedroom (over the parlor), and a porch. The loft in the original part of the house served as a second upstairs bedroom. A dining room is now located behind the bedroom/sitting room. It is believed that this room was not part of the Washington house, but was added by a later owner. Another post-Washington addition, built in about 1800 on the other side of the parlor, now holds a gift shop.

Mary Washington lived in the house for the last seventeen years of her life. Her son visited her for the last time in 1789 and received her blessing prior to traveling to New York for his first presidential inauguration. She died later that year at the age of eighty-one.

After Mrs. Washington's death, her daughter sold the house, which then changed hands a number of times over the years. In 1889, someone overheard the owner discussing the possibility of selling the house and having it dismantled and shipped to Chicago for the Columbian Exposition. A concerned Fredericksburg resident notified the newly formed Association for the Preservation of Virginia Antiquities (now APVA Preservation Virginia), which was able to purchase the historic house. The APVA restored the home to its eighteenth-century appearance and furnished it with fine period pieces. The Mary Washington Branch of the APVA manages the property, which is open for tours most days of the year.

Mary Washington's house is simple but stylish. The parlor is the best room in the house, with special features such as finely carved cornices and lower paneling on the walls. The lovely fireplace mantel was a gift from George Washington to his mother. When he built the addition, Washington added closets to this room and to the bedroom above it, a feature that was still uncommon in colonial America. The bedroom/sitting room is where Mrs. Washington spent most of her time and visited with close acquaintances and family. This is the room in which she last visited with her son and told him goodbye, and the room in which she died.

Behind the house, the eighteenth-century quarters kitchen still stands, as do the large boxwoods that are thought to have been planted during Mary Washington's time. In the cottage-type garden, which was re-created by the Garden Club of Virginia in 1969, a colorful collage of flowers, flowering trees, and shrubs is accessed by a brick walk system. A sundial base believed to have been Mrs. Washington's stands in the center.

FACING PAGE: *Mary Ball Washington lived the last seventeen years of her life in this comfortable but modest Fredericksburg house that was bought for her by her son, George, in 1772. It was within a short walking distance of Kenmore, the home of her daughter, Betty Lewis.*

TOP: *When George Washington bought the house, this area was two separate rooms. He knocked down the wall between the rooms and turned it into one large bedroom/sitting room for his mother. Before attending his presidential inauguration in 1789, George Washington visited with his mother for the last time in this room.*

Kenmore

1201 WASHINGTON AVENUE
FREDERICKSBURG, VA 22401

Fielding Lewis was a wealthy eighteenth-century planter and merchant, a prominent Spotsylvania County citizen, and a representative to the Virginia House of Burgesses. In 1775, he and his second wife (and second cousin), Betty Washington, sister of George Washington, moved into their newly completed mansion on his 1,270-acre wheat, corn, and tobacco plantation. Situated just outside of the village of Fredericksburg (now within the city), the bustling plantation, which fronted on the Rappahannock River, also included a store and a busy shipyard.

The Lewises moved into their stylish new home just when the colonies were on the brink of revolution. Once the Revolutionary War began, Fielding Lewis, a true patriot, did everything in his power to help the war effort, including providing food and supplies to his brother-in-law's army as well as using and exhausting his personal fortune to build and operate the Fredericksburg Gunnery. In December 1781, just weeks after the surrender at Yorktown, Lewis died, impoverished.

After Lewis' death, Betty remained in the mansion, struggling to get by, for fourteen years. After her death in 1797, her stepson, John Lewis, sold the plantation. Over the years, it changed hands many times, and the acreage was divided up and sold off. The Gordon family, who purchased the property in 1819, named it Kenmore, after their ancestral home in Scotland. The house suffered heavy damage during the Civil War, as it was struck by cannon balls from both sides during the Battle of Fredericksburg. Later, it was used as a Union hospital after the Battle of the Wilderness.

In 1925, the Kenmore Association (now the George Washington Foundation), consisting of

ABOVE: *From Kenmore's entry passage, an elaborate staircase provides access to four bedchambers on the second floor. Research revealed that the passage was originally painted a vivid yellow ochre.*

FACING PAGE: *Although it currently stands on 3 acres in the middle of Old Town Fredericksburg, when it was built in the 1770s, Kenmore was the manor house of a 1,270-acre plantation located just outside of town. The brick Georgian mansion, seen here from the west front, was the home of Fielding Lewis and his second wife, Betty Washington Lewis, and four of their eight surviving children.*

a group of Fredericksburg residents led by Mrs. Vivian Minor Fleming, saved Kenmore from being demolished or converted into apartments by its last private owner, "Peck" Heflin. After raising $30,000 to meet Heflin's asking price, the group acquired the house, began restoration, and opened it to the public. The house, which stands on 3 acres, is now open daily all year.

The elegant Georgian-style dwelling with its four tall chimneys faces out across a sprawling, tree-covered lawn that is enclosed by a brick wall. The two-story house with full basement is built of brick laid in Flemish bond. A Federal-style portico on the back of the house was added in the 1800s. Inside, the house has four rooms and a passage on each floor, but the floor plan, unlike most Georgian dwellings, is not arranged symmetrically.

In contrast to its dignified and sober exterior, Kenmore's interior is bright and opulent. Based on research and architectural evidence, a multiyear restoration project completed in April 2008 corrected inaccurate paint colors and wallpapers. Previous subdued shades of peach, white, and gray have been replaced by vibrant colors like yellow ochre and Prussian blue, and authentic reproductions of the exquisite Lewis wallpapers now cover the walls.

Kenmore's most notable features are its outstanding plasterwork ceilings and overmantels, which were created by a highly talented eighteenth-century artisan known only as the "stucco man." The drawing room's ceiling design depicts the seasons of the year, while the chamber features a classical mask of the Greek sun god, Apollo. In the dining room, the home's largest and most important public room, an incredible plasterwork overmantel portrays "The Fox and the Crow" from *Aesop's Fables*. All of the plasterwork ceilings, overmantels, and cornices were meticulously cleaned, restored, and whitewashed during the recent restoration.

The Garden Club of Virginia held its first Historic Garden Week in 1929, and the proceeds went toward its first restoration project—the gardens at Kenmore. In 1992, the club's landscape architects redesigned the formal eighteenth-century gardens at the rear of the house. The design, which features a foursquare garden planted with a variety of perennials and lined with boxwood, is conjectural, since no records or archeological data were available. In 1992, a Wilderness Walk was added to the property's southwest corner, which includes an array of native American plantings, including dogwood, mountain laurel, bluebells, and columbine. The gardens are lovingly cared for by the volunteer members of the Kenmore Garden Guild.

FACING PAGE: *The dining room, one of three rooms that boasts magnificent plasterwork, features this intricate overmantel depicting "The Fox and the Crow" from Aesop's Fables. A crow sits in a tree with a piece of cheese in its mouth. The fox, standing under the tree, tricks the crow into dropping the cheese by asking him to sing.*

RIGHT: *In the drawing room, each of the ceiling's four corners represents a different season of the year in masterful plasterwork. The designs were chosen from English pattern books and created by a talented artisan known only as the "stucco man." The room's original eighteenth-century wool-flocked wallpaper was reproduced in a complex process in which varnish is used to adhere chopped wool to the paper's surface.*

BELOW: *The back of the mansion at Kenmore overlooks a large, terraced foursquare garden edged in boxwood. Adjacent to the parterre, a small walled cutting garden, with a center sundial, is filled with spring flowers, including the prolific white candytuft columbine. The Federal-style portico on the back of the house was added in the 1800s.*

Gunston Hall

10709 GUNSTON ROAD
MASON NECK, VA 22079

Gunston Hall was the home of one of America's most influential founding fathers, George Mason. The house was the center of a 5,500-acre tobacco and wheat plantation situated on a peninsula on the Potomac River, just south of Alexandria.

Although he was a man of great intellect, wisdom, and character, Mason, unlike his friends and peers Thomas Jefferson, George Washington, and James Madison, had no desire to hold public office. But when Washington was named chief of the Continental army, Mason reluctantly agreed to take his seat in the Virginia legislature.

At the Virginia Convention in 1776, Mason was called on to draft a declaration of rights and a state constitution to allow Virginia to act as an independent political body. Mason's Virginia Declaration of Rights detailed the rights and liberties of individual citizens, pronouncing "That all men are by nature equally free and independent and have certain inherent rights . . . [among which are] the enjoyment of life and liberty." Mason's document would later influence Thomas Jefferson in his penning of the Declaration of Independence.

In 1787, at the Constitutional Convention in Philadelphia, Mason refused to sign the new Constitution, which he argued gave too much power to the federal government and did not address the rights of individuals. James Madison eventually convinced the first Congress to modify the Constitution. Based on Mason's Virginia Declaration of Rights, the first ten amendments—called the U.S. Bill of Rights—were added to the Constitution.

RIGHT: *Gunston Hall was the manor house of a 5,500-acre tobacco and wheat plantation on the Potomac River. The one-and-a-half-story Georgian home was built in 1755 by prominent Virginia statesman George Mason, author of the Virginia Declaration of Rights. Today, the home's 550 scenic acres include a farmyard with period animals, a deer park, nature trails, and the Mason family graveyard.*

FACING PAGE: *A grand stairway rises from the wide central passage to the second floor, which contains seven bedchambers and a storage room. At the top of the stairs is a graceful three-part arch with fluted pillars. On the first floor, a double arch with a centered carved pine-cone pendant divides the front and back halls.*

Mason began construction on Gunston Hall in 1755. The house is a one-and-a-half story Georgian-style structure with gable ends. It is built of brick laid in Flemish bond. Classical features—including a cornice, a pedimented Palladian doorway, and stone blocks called quoins outlining the corners of the house—all proclaim the status and wealth of the home's owner. Inside, the ground floor is laid out in the traditional Georgian style, with four large rooms (parlor, dining room, master bedchamber, and study) and a spacious central hall. Deviating from the traditional plan, however, the second floor holds seven bedchambers and a storage room. The additional bedrooms were needed for Mason's large family, which included nine children.

A young Englishman named William Buckland, who trained in London as a carpenter/joiner, came to America as Mason's indentured servant. He directed the mansion's construction and is credited with designing the elaborately ornamented interiors for which Gunston Hall is most noted. Using Buckland's designs, carver William Bernard Sears, another indentured servant, crafted the magnificent carved woodwork. The stylishness, beauty, and masterful workmanship of Gunston Hall's formal rooms far surpass that found in most colonial American homes.

Upon entering the wide central hallway, visitors are immediately impressed by its Doric-style fluted pilasters, intricately carved entablature, and the double elliptical arch with a centered, carved pine-cone pendant that divides the front and back halls. The dining room is the most elaborate room in the house, with lavish classical woodwork that shows hints of rococo design. Dominating one wall is an ornately carved chimney breast, flanked on either side by built-in beaufats. The parlor is both unique and stunning, boldly painted in yellow ochre with chinoiserie, or Chinese-style woodwork.

Mason lived at Gunston Hall until his death in 1792. It then remained in the Mason family until 1866. Its last private owners, Mr. and Mrs. Louis Hertle, bequeathed it to the Commonwealth of Virginia upon Mr. Hertle's death in 1949. As stipulated by Hertle, the site is open to the public as a museum and is governed by a board of regents, the members of which are appointed from the

National Society of the Colonial Dames of America. Gunston Hall is open daily, year round.

The painstakingly restored mansion and its reconstructed outbuildings are set on 550 beautiful acres on the Potomac River. Its garden is currently in a transitional stage, as the remains of a mid-twentieth-century colonial revival garden are being replaced by an authentic eighteenth-century garden based on archaeological findings. A central allée of English boxwood, planted by George Mason, still survives.

FACING PAGE: *The lavish classical rococo-style woodwork makes the dining room the finest room in the house. One wall is dominated by an intricately carved chimneybreast that is flanked by two built-in cupboards called beaufats. All three features are crowned by classical broken pediments.*

TOP: *Featuring flamboyant wallpaper, vivid yellow ochre paint, and chinoiserie (Chinese-style woodwork) in the mantel, overdoors, and windows, Gunston Hall's parlor was bold, exciting, and quite unlike any other rooms in colonial America.*

RIGHT: *The little parlor served as Mason's study as well as the family's informal dining room and parlor. Compared to the ornate public rooms, this private space is much more modest. Furnishings in the room include Mason's small writing table, where it is believed he did most of his work.*

Woodlawn Plantation

9000 RICHMOND HIGHWAY
ALEXANDRIA, VA 22309

Perched on a hilltop some 3 miles from George Washington's Mount Vernon Estate is Woodlawn Plantation, home of Major Lawrence Lewis and his wife, Eleanor "Nelly" Parke Custis.

Nelly Custis was the granddaughter of George Washington's wife, Martha. In 1781, Nelly was less than three years old when her father, John Parke Custis (Martha's son from her first marriage), died. Nelly and her younger brother then went to live at Mount Vernon as the foster children of their dear "Grandmama and Grandpapa." Lawrence Lewis was the nephew of George Washington— the son of Washington's sister, Betty, and her husband, Fielding Lewis, of Fredericksburg. When Washington retired to Mount Vernon in 1797 at the end of his presidency, he found himself constantly entertaining visitors, including military officers, cabinet members, politicians, and foreign dignitaries. He asked Lawrence to come to Mount Vernon to assist him as his secretary and host. Once there, Lawrence soon won the affections of young Nelly, and the two were married at Mount Vernon on February 22, 1799, Washington's last birthday.

Washington gifted 2,000 acres of his Mount Vernon estate to the couple and recommended a spot on a hill, which had a broad view of the Potomac and of Mount Vernon, as the ideal location for their home. He then asked William Thornton, the first architect of the U.S. Capitol building, to design their house. Unfortunately, Washington died before construction could begin.

The Lewises were still living at Mount Vernon with Nelly's grandmother when construction on the mansion started in 1800. Martha Washington died in May 1802, and by the end of that year,

Nelly, Lawrence, and their three-year-old daughter had moved into their still-unfinished mansion.

The elegant late Georgian/early Federal-style mansion, completed in 1805, incorporates a five-part Palladian-plan. The dwelling consists of a two-story central block with one-and-a-half story dependency wings on each side. The wings are connected to the house by enclosed hyphens. (Originally one-story, the hyphens were raised to their present height in the early 1900s.) The house is built of brick fired on the plantation. The stone aprons, water table, and other exterior decorative trim were made from local Aquia sandstone.

The central portion of the house features the traditional four-over-four plan with two large rooms on either side of a wide central hallway. The ground floor holds a parlor, a music room, a dining room, and a master bedchamber. The spacious hallway with double doors at each end features a graceful winding staircase that ascends to the second floor, where there are four bedchambers. Rooms throughout the house are embellished with fine Adamesque woodwork and plaster designs, and many of the furnishings and art objects are Lewis and Washington family pieces.

The home's north wing held an office and a servants' hall, while the south wing contained a kitchen and washhouse. Connected to these wings are a meat house and a dairy.

Of the eight children born to the Lewises, only three survived past childhood, two of whom predeceased Nelly. When Lawrence died in 1839, their son Lorenzo inherited Woodlawn. Lorenzo, who owned an estate in Clarke County, moved his mother in with his family, leaving Woodlawn empty until it was sold in 1846. Over the next century, it passed through several owners and alternating periods of deterioration and renewal before the nonprofit Woodlawn Public Foundation purchased it in 1949. Two years later, Woodlawn became the first site administered by the National Trust for Historic Preservation. That organization restored the property and opened it to the public as a historic house museum. It is open March through December.

In 1953, the Garden Club of Virginia began a refurbishment of Woodlawn's gardens and grounds, which have been modified over the years. Two parterres in the formal garden hold various plantings. Dividing the garden is a long allée of golden raintrees with a border of flowers and herbs beneath them. The irregular border of the mansion's sweeping front lawn is a serpentine pathway lined with flowers and flowering trees and shrubs, including azaleas and hydrangeas.

FACING PAGE: *George Washington gifted 2,000 acres of his Mount Vernon estate to his nephew, Lawrence Lewis, and step-granddaughter, Nelly Custis, as a wedding present. He recommended the site for a house, calling it "a most beautiful site for a gentleman's seat." In 1800, construction began on the elegant Federal-style plantation house, designed by famed architect William Thornton.*

RIGHT: *Beautiful golden raintrees adorn the Formal Garden at Woodlawn. The garden is composed of two parterres, accessed by crisscrossing walkways.*

ABOVE: *Woodlawn's enchanting Formal Garden is a popular venue for weddings. After entering through picturesque garden gates, a brick walkway runs through a long allée of golden raintrees.*

RIGHT: *Colorful pink and blue hydrangeas beautify the path of Woodlawn's Serpentine Garden. In spring, the garden is decked out in vibrant azaleas.*

ABOVE: *Located on the mansion's first floor, the master bedchamber features original Lewis furnishings, including the bed and desk.*

LEFT: *Since music was very important in the Lewis family, it is logical that the largest and most fashionable room in the house is identified as the music room. The room contains many elaborate features, such as the beautifully carved Italian fireplace mantel.*

Mount Vernon

3200 MOUNT VERNON
MEMORIAL HIGHWAY
MOUNT VERNON, VA 22121

George Washington—"first in war, first in peace, and first in the hearts of his countrymen," as described in a eulogy written by Henry Lee—was and will forever remain the supreme hero of an adoring nation. A man of great integrity, character, and unwavering devotion to his country, he was a brilliant military leader who went on to guide an infant democracy through its first shaky steps. Yet despite a career filled with grand accomplishments, he humbly stated that his most important occupation in life was that of a farmer. Indeed, his happiest years were those spent as a gentleman farmer at his beloved Mount Vernon.

Mount Vernon, which was originally known as Little Hunting Creek Plantation, became the seat of the Washington family when George's great-grandfather John Washington acquired it in 1674. After the death of his father, Augustine, in 1743, George spent much of his youth at Mount Vernon with his older half-brother, Lawrence, who had received the estate from Augustine. George subsequently inherited the plantation when Lawrence died.

Washington lived at Mount Vernon from 1754 until his death in 1799, except for those years spent serving his country. Each time he returned home, he intended never again to serve in public life, but duty kept calling. He devoted thirteen years to military service, first in the French and Indian War and later the Revolutionary War. He spent months presiding over the Constitutional Convention and championing the Constitution's ratification, and then served eight years as president. Finally, in 1797, at the end of his presidency, he retired permanently to Mount Vernon but, sadly, died less than three years later at the age of sixty-seven.

In 1853, a group of women determined to save Mount Vernon as a national shrine founded the Mount Vernon Ladies' Association and began raising funds for its purchase. In 1858, they acquired the mansion, its outbuildings, and 200 acres (the property now includes 500) from the Washington family. With the goal of restoring the mansion to its 1799 appearance, the association opened it and the grounds to the public in 1860. It is open every day of the year.

During his forty-five-year residency, Washington increased the plantation's size from 2,000 to 8,000 acres. It was divided into five separate farms, each with its own overseer, buildings, and work force. A very innovative farmer, Washington continually experimented with new techniques, crops, and fertilizers. He also diversified into other areas, including livestock breeding, milling, and a distillery business.

Washington's father built the central portion of the present mansion in about 1735. When Washington inherited the house, it was a modest one-and-a-half-story structure with four rooms and a central hall. Using his own creative vision and a large architectural library, Washington enlarged and renovated the mansion, turning it into one of America's most elegant eighteenth-century homes. By the time he finished in 1787, the spacious mansion contained twenty-one rooms.

ABOVE: *As the sun rises over the Potomac River, it casts a warm glow on the east front of George Washington's Mount Vernon. Washington added the striking high-columned piazza to the house in about 1777. From there, he could enjoy a panoramic view of the Potomac. He also added the cupola and "dove of peace" weathervane that have become some of the home's most distinguishing features.*

RIGHT: *Irises and other colorful perennials bloom along the path in Mount Vernon's Upper Garden. In 1785, Washington turned this garden, which had previously contained fruit and nut trees, into a pleasure garden filled primarily with flowers. Today it contains plantings specifically mentioned by Washington, as well as others from the eighteenth century.*

Around 1757, Washington began expanding his home by raising it to two-and-a-half stories. He needed that extra space in 1759 when he married Martha Dandridge Custis, a widow with two children. By 1774, he began construction of a south wing, which contains the master bedchamber and study. That was followed by a north wing, which holds the large two-story dining room with its magnificent Palladian-style window. He beveled the mansion's wood siding to give the appearance of stone and then applied sand to the painted surface—a treatment known as rustication. He later added the columned piazza on the east facade and the hexagonal cupola with its "dove of peace" weathervane.

Washington embellished the interior with paneling, cornice molding and chair rails, ornate mantels and overmantels, intricate plasterwork designs on the ceilings, and classical pediments over the doorways. Rooms were papered and painted in rich, vibrant colors like Prussian blue and verdigris green. In the large passage, he added a graceful walnut staircase. The ceiling of the small dining room features decorative plasterwork fashioned by the same talented "stucco man" who had created the fabulous designs at Kenmore, the Fredericksburg home of Washington's sister, Betty.

In the landscaping of the grounds around the mansion, Washington brought numerous elements together to create a tranquil setting that was both beautiful and functional. On the western side of the house is a large, grassy bowling green, which is bordered by a serpentine walkway and tree groupings. Symmetrically placed on each side of the bowling green are two large, brick-walled, shield-shaped gardens. The lower (kitchen) garden contains beds of vegetables and herbs, with fruit trees espaliered along its walls. Washington made the upper garden a colorful pleasure garden, filling it primarily with flowers. Its beds, which were restored to their original size based on archaeological excavations, contain plantings mentioned by Washington in his records, as well as other eighteenth-century varieties. Washington also grew a variety of exotic plants and trees in his greenhouse, which burned in 1835. The present structure, on the same site, is a reconstruction of the original.

ABOVE: *The lower (or kitchen) garden supplied the fruit and produce for Mount Vernon during Washington's times. Today, the vegetables and herbs that fill the beds and the fruit trees that are espaliered along the garden's walls are all varieties mentioned in Washington's writings and in the reports of his gardener.*

LEFT: *In 1785, Washington built a greenhouse where he and his gardeners experimented with exotic plants, including tropical and semi-tropical varieties such as orange, lemon, lime, and coffee. The greenhouse was flanked on each side by slave quarters. The complex burned in 1835 and was rebuilt on its original site in 1951. It fronts two formal re-created boxwood parterres designed in the shape of a French fleur-de-lis.*

FACING PAGE: *The west front of Mount Vernon faces out over a courtyard. Two dependencies—a kitchen and servants hall—are connected to the mansion by covered walkways called colonnades. Beyond the courtyard is an expansive bowling green. During Washington's forty-five years at Mount Vernon, he increased the mansion's size from four to twenty-one rooms and the plantation's acreage from 2,000 to 8,000 acres.*

ABOVE: The west parlor, painted in a rich Prussian blue, is one of the most architecturally important rooms at Mount Vernon, with its fully paneled walls, classical Palladian door frames, and ornately carved fireplace mantel. A carved Washington family coat of arms is displayed in the pediment over the mantel. The room was used for family gatherings as well as for entertaining guests.

LEFT: Washington's last addition to the house was the two-story large dining room. A vision in verdigris green, the stunning room is adorned with magnificent plaster ornamentation and a spectacular Palladian window. The Washingtons entertained large numbers of guests in the room, and it was here, in April 1789, that Washington was informed that he had been elected the nation's first president.

ABOVE: Washington turned a small bedchamber on the first floor into the little parlor, which was used regularly by the family for musical entertainment. A harpsichord that Washington ordered from London in 1793 for his step-granddaughter, Nelly Custis, is the centerpiece of the room.

RIGHT: George and Martha Washington's second-floor bedchamber is located in the private south wing. Washington died here, in this bed, on December 14, 1799, from a throat infection identified as quinsy. After his death, Martha Washington closed this room and made a small room on the third floor her bedchamber for the remainder of her life.

Carlyle House

121 NORTH FAIRFAX STREET
ALEXANDRIA, VA 22314

In 1741, twenty-one-year-old John Carlyle left his home in Scotland bound for Virginia, where he was to be a colonial representative for the English tobacco merchant William Hicks. His ambition and shrewd business skills quickly gained him financial success. That success was further strengthened by his fortuitous marriage to Sarah Fairfax, a member of one of colonial Virginia's most prestigious families. William Fairfax, Carlyle's father-in-law, was the land agent and cousin of Thomas, the sixth Lord Fairfax. Carlyle's brother-in-law was Lawrence Washington, the older half brother of George Washington. With his large land holdings and numerous business interests, which included import and export trade abroad and retail trade in Alexandria, Carlyle ultimately became one of the wealthiest and most prominent men in Virginia.

Carlyle was one of the cofounders of Alexandria, and in 1749, he bought two of the best lots in the new city. Located between the Potomac River and the market square, the site was the ideal location for his home and his merchant business. In 1751, construction began on his magnificent new mansion. He and Sarah moved into the house on August 1, 1753, and that same evening, Sarah gave birth to their first son.

Carlyle's stunning, self-designed, Georgian-Palladian mansion was most unusual at the time of its construction. It was built of local Aquia sandstone when most other houses were made of wood. It was also much larger and grander in finish than most houses in colonial Virginia. Dominating the town with its size and opulence, the mansion was an important visible symbol of Carlyle's wealth and prominence.

The home's interior, with its rich architectural detail, is also a statement in grandeur. With a typical eighteenth-century floor plan, the two-story house features a wide center hall flanked by two rooms on either side. Downstairs, the center passage separates the public rooms (parlor, dining room) from the private (master bedchamber, study). The second floor holds four bedchambers. The largest room in the house, the dining room, is also the most striking, since this is where the family entertained their many important guests. The intricate wood carving, all of which is original, is superb. The wide carved cornice and chair rail, the carved pediments above the doors, and the delicate egg-and-dart wood trim that surrounds the fireplace's marble inset are all expensive embellishments, intended to impress.

In 1755, when General Edward Braddock was sent to Virginia by King George III to oversee the escalating French and Indian War, he selected Carlyle's mansion as his headquarters. He called a conference of five colonial governors to meet there to plan the early campaigns of the war, and the Carlyles' lovely dining room became their meeting room. For years after this legendary conference, Carlyle's home was called the Braddock House.

FACING PAGE: *Built in 1753, Carlyle House was the grand Georgian-Palladian home of wealthy merchant John Carlyle, one of the cofounders of the city of Alexandria. At the time of the mansion's construction, only two percent of houses in the Virginia colony were comparable in size and grandeur.*

RIGHT: *The wood trim surrounding the dining room fireplace's marble inset is carved in an egg-and-dart motif, a popular design of the period that symbolized the beginning and end of life.*

Sarah Carlyle died in 1761, leaving John with two small daughters. He had a son from his second wife, Sybil West, though Sybil died after ten years of marriage. Carlyle's son, George William, inherited the mansion when his father died in 1780. After George William died the following year, the family of Carlyle's only surviving child, Sarah Carlyle Herbert, occupied the mansion until her death in 1827, at which time her son sold it. For more than a century, it had many owners and served as a hotel and a Civil War hospital as well as a private residence. In 1970, the Northern Virginia Regional Park Authority acquired the badly deteriorated mansion and restored it to its original eighteenth-century appearance. The house and gardens were opened to the public in 1976 as the Carlyle House Historic Park. The property is open all year, Tuesday through Sunday.

A three-quarter-acre re-created garden is filled with carefully researched plantings that would have been available to John Carlyle during his occupancy. It features boxwood parterres, a cutting garden, and flowering trees and shrubs. With its charming gazebo and inviting benches, this open green space offers visitors an oasis of solitude and tranquility right in the center of Old Town Alexandria.

TOP: *The dining room was the most public and most impressive room in John Carlyle's home. The quality and workmanship are evident in such features as the wide carved cornice, the fully paneled walls, and the classical carved pediments above the doors. In 1755, General Edward Braddock used this room as his conference room when he met with five colonial governors to strategize during the French and Indian War.*

LEFT: *The small parlor, with its vivid green wallpaper and stylish floor covering, was used by the Carlyle family for leisure activities such as reading, card playing, and musical entertainment.*

BELOW: *With flowering trees and shrubs, a variety of colorful flowers, and a charming gazebo, the re-created eighteenth-century garden at the rear of the Carlyle House offers a cool and tranquil retreat in the middle of Old Town Alexandria.*

Oatlands Plantation

20850 PLANTATION LANE
LEESBURG, VA 20175

George Carter, a great-grandson of the wealthy and powerful Robert "King" Carter, was a twenty-year-old bachelor when he inherited 3,408 acres of Loudoun County farmland from his father in 1798, on which he started a wheat plantation. In 1804, he began constructing a manor house on his plantation, which he called Oatlands.

It is believed that Carter designed the house himself using pattern books. His original plan was a Federal-style dwelling that featured symmetrical east and west bays on either side of a central block. Built of brick fired on the property, the three-story mansion had a small attic and a full basement. By 1808, some of the rooms on the first floor had been finished, but the upper floors were just framed in. It was then that various events and circumstances caused construction on the mansion to stop.

By the 1820s, when Carter was finally ready to resume construction, styles as well as his tastes had changed. He altered his Federal-style mansion to reflect the Greek Revival style that was popular in the country at the time. He covered the exterior red brick walls with stucco made of sand, horse-hair, and crushed limestone. It was then scored to resemble stone and painted a cream color. He erected a striking front portico with two-story columns topped with elaborately carved Corinthian capitals. A parapet wall, which he constructed along the front and side rooflines, further enhanced the mansion's visual appeal. Half-octagonal wings with staircases were added on either end. Inside, Carter enclosed two corners of his drawing room to form an octagon, which was quite a fashionable shape in the early 1800s. He embellished the interiors with intricately detailed plasterwork and finely carved woodwork in the Adamesque and Greek Revival styles.

Over the years, as Carter's plantation flourished, he added numerous outbuildings to the property, such as a smokehouse, a three-story bank barn, a dairy, and a propagation greenhouse. Near the mansion, he designed and built a large, walled, multi-terraced garden as well as various garden dependencies.

At the age of fifty-eight, Carter married Elizabeth Grayson, with whom he had two sons. After he died in 1846, she managed the plantation and raised their children. George Carter II and his wife, Katherine, occupied Oatlands during and after the Civil War. Left with large debts and an absence of slave labor, the family's fortunes declined after the war. For a time, George and Katherine operated Oatlands as a girls' school and later as a summer boarding house.

In 1897, the Carter family sold the mansion and 60 acres to Stilson Hutchins, founder of the *Washington Post*. Stilson sold it in 1903 to wealthy Washingtonians William and Edith Eustis. They completed a beautiful and sensitive restoration that made very few changes to the original Carter floor plan and architectural features.

Although George Carter's gardens had been sadly neglected for years, Edith Eustis, a passionate gardener, recognized their hidden beauty and potential, and under her care, they blossomed. As

FACING PAGE: *George Carter began building a Federal-style manor home at his 3,400-acre Oatlands Plantation in 1804 but stopped before its completion. When construction resumed in the 1820s, Carter altered the design to reflect the Greek Revival style that was then in vogue, adding the columned front portico, parapet wall, and two half-octagonal wings. The red brick exterior was covered with stucco and painted.*

RIGHT: *In Oatlands' garden, the sculpture Young Faun, a creation of Italian-American sculptor Attilio Piccirilli, looks out over the reflecting pool, which Edith Eustis had built in the 1930s. Beyond the pool, at the end of a long allée of boxwood, stands her teahouse.*

designed by Carter, the garden features a series of terraces that are cut into the hillside and accessed by steps and walkways. He filled the level areas of the terraces with vegetables, flowers, and other plantings. With creative flair, Eustis transformed the neglected garden into a thing of beauty, filling the terraces with boxwood-lined parterres bursting with colorful tulips, peonies, irises, and lilies. She added interesting statuary and other garden structures such as a teahouse, as well as a bowling green, a reflecting pool, and a rose garden. Many plantings from the Carter era survive, including American and English boxwood, a European larch tree, and a majestic English oak.

After Edith Eustis died in 1964, her daughters, Margaret Eustis Finley and Anne Eustis Emmett, donated the mansion, its furnishings, and 261 acres to the National Trust for Historic Preservation. Today, Oatlands, a National Trust for Historic Preservation site, is managed by Oatlands Inc., a local, self-supporting nonprofit organization. The property is open for tours April through December.

TOP: *Colorful peonies and irises put on a springtime show at Oatlands. The sumptuous multi-terraced gardens, originally designed and built by George Carter and then transformed by Edith Eustis, are filled with boxwood-lined parterres holding a large assortment of flowers from early spring through autumn.*

FACING PAGE, TOP: *The large entry hall of the Oatlands Plantation home contains elaborate decorations such as the carved arched doorway and intricately detailed plaster cornice. Adorning the wall is a full-length portrait of Louise Eustis, the mother of William Eustis, who purchased Oatlands in 1903.*

FACING PAGE, BOTTOM: *In the early 1820s, Carter enclosed two corners of his drawing room to create an octagon, a defining shape of Jeffersonian architecture, which was popular in the early nineteenth century. A portrait of Edith Eustis, painted by a French artist, hangs over the desk.*

ABOVE: *When completed in 1813, Virginia's Executive Mansion, or "state house" as it was called then, was the finest governor's residence in the nation. During the Civil War, a bucket brigade saved the mansion and the Capitol from a fire that consumed much of Richmond when the city fell to Union troops in 1865.*

Part III

CAPITAL REGION
&
CENTRAL VIRGINIA

Virginia's Executive Mansion

CAPITOL SQUARE
203 GOVERNOR STREET
RICHMOND, VA 23219

The Executive Mansion in Richmond is the oldest continuously occupied governor's residence in the nation. The handsome mansion, which is Virginia's third state-owned governor's residence since 1776, has been the home of the Commonwealth's governors and their families as well as the center of official entertaining since its completion in 1813.

Virginia's first two governors, Patrick Henry and Thomas Jefferson, resided at the Governor's Palace in Williamsburg. After Governor Jefferson moved the state capital to Richmond in 1780, he and subsequent governors lived in rental properties until the late 1700s, when a governor's residence was built in Capitol Square adjacent to the new State Capitol building. That modest frame dwelling, which stood near the site of the present mansion, served as the residence for twelve administrations. In 1811, after Governor John Tyler Sr. complained to the Legislature that the house was intolerable, the General Assembly approved the building of the Commonwealth's third and current governor's residence. In 1813, Governor James Barbour and his family became the first residents of the new mansion.

Constructed of brick laid in Flemish bond, the house is an excellent example of Federal-style architecture. Originally, the dwelling had two simple side porches but no front porch. By the 1830s, its attractive but rather plain façade had been greatly enhanced by the construction of a wooden balustrade that connected its four chimneys, parapets above its eaves, and a front porch.

Designed by architect Alexander Parris, the first floor of the two-story mansion originally had a broad entrance hall that was flanked by four rooms (governor's office, ladies' parlor,

ABOVE: *The room is reflected in the glass of a wall mirror that hangs in the entrance hall of the Executive Mansion.*

dining room, and parlor). Rather than a grand stairway, the house had two staircases, located in corridors on opposite sides of the hall. One was for the servants, and another, more formal one was for the family's use. Upstairs were four bedrooms and a storeroom.

In 1906, an addition and renovations designed by prominent Virginia architect Duncan Lee increased the size and grandeur of the mansion. The original back parlor and dining room were combined to form one large ballroom for entertaining, and an oval-shaped formal state dining room was built at the rear of the house. Over the years, numerous other structural and decorative additions and modifications were made to make the residence more attractive as well as more functional and comfortable for its inhabitants. These included the expansion of the upstairs private living quarters to five bedrooms, a den, a study, and a small kitchen.

The first-floor public rooms are open for tours Tuesday through Thursday. They include the old governor's office and ladies' parlor, which have been faithfully restored to reflect their early nineteenth-century appearance and contain mostly original woodwork, plaster cornices, and ornamental ceilings, as well as the grand center ballroom and the elegant oval dining room.

When visitors step through the front door into the expansive 15-foot-high entry hall, their eyes are immediately drawn through a sequence of gracefully carved arches to the formal dining room at the end of the long hallway. There, hanging prominently on the dining room wall, is a late-sixteenth-century portrait of a woman believed to be Queen Elizabeth I, the Virgin Queen, for whom Virginia was named.

In 1999, the Garden Club of Virginia restored the mansion's lovely south garden, planting it in shrubs and colorful perennials. The well-known Richmond landscape architect Charles Gillette originally designed the garden for Governor and Mrs. Thomas Stanley in 1954. The Garden Club was guided in their restoration efforts by Gillette's original plans and records as well as by photographs that were taken at the original garden's opening.

ABOVE: *An impressive view greets those entering the Executive Mansion. Their eyes travel down a long expanse from the grand entrance hall through a succession of graceful archways to the ballroom and the formal dining room beyond. An elegant neoclassical cornice crowns the lofty 15-foot-high entrance hall.*

RIGHT: *During renovations made in 1906, the wall was removed between the original mansion's parlor and dining room, and the two rooms were combined to form one large ballroom. It serves as the primary entertainment area for the mansion.*

FACING PAGE: *Noted Richmond landscape architect Charles Gillette originally designed the Executive Mansion's south garden in 1954. The Garden Club of Virginia referred to Gillette's original records when it undertook a restoration of the garden in 1999. Spring finds the garden abloom with tulips and other colorful perennials.*

The John Marshall House

818 EAST MARSHALL STREET
RICHMOND, VA 23219

Born in a log cabin in 1755 in what was then still the Virginia frontier, John Marshall rose to become the fourth and most influential Chief Justice of the United States Supreme Court.

After a childhood education that consisted of home schooling plus one year at Campbell Academy in Westmoreland County, Marshall planned to pursue a law career. However, his plans were put on hold in 1775 when, at the age of twenty, he joined the Continental army and served as an officer in the Revolutionary War.

Returning to Virginia in 1779, Marshall resumed his legal education, which was limited to private study plus a short study of law at the College of William and Mary in 1780. Remarkably, he passed the bar examination that very same year. In 1783, Marshall and his bride, Mary Willis Ambler, whom he called "my dearest Polly," moved to Richmond, Virginia's state capital since 1780. There he established a successful law practice.

In 1788, the Marshalls began building a house in Richmond's Court End, a fashionable neighborhood located close to Court Square. Marshall had purchased four lots that composed a square, or entire city block. Eventually, his in-town estate included the house, a law office, a kitchen, a laundry, a carriage house, and a garden.

ABOVE: *Chief Justice John Marshall's handsome Federal-style mansion stands in downtown Richmond's Court End, close to the Capitol. Completed in 1790, it was home to Marshall, his beloved wife, Mary, and their six children. Marshall remained in his Richmond home until his death in 1835.*

Completed in 1790, the house is a striking two-story dwelling built of brick laid in Flemish bond. Primarily Federal in style, it also features Georgian elements such as the English-bond brick water table and paneled interior walls and wainscoting. The house has a four-over-four floor plan, with the fourth room being a hall passage located at the rear of the home. It opens into the parlor and large dining room and provides stair access to the three upstairs bedchambers as well as to the outbuildings behind the house. This is unlike most Federal homes, whose rooms typically lie to each side of a central passage that runs the length of the house.

The neoclassically decorated dining room, the home's largest and most formal room, was designed and furnished to allow for a variety of uses. It served as the center of the many large social events held by the Marshalls. Adjacent to this room is a smaller dining room, used for family dining as well as for additional entertaining space for large gatherings. The withdrawing room, or parlor, was where the ladies would retire after dinner, leaving the dining room to the gentlemen. All three of these public rooms were elaborately decorated and furnished to impress their visitors.

Marshall served four terms in the Virginia House of Delegates and was elected to the U.S. House of Representatives in 1799. President John Adams appointed him secretary of state in 1800 and then nominated him in 1801 to be the fourth Chief Justice of the Supreme Court, a position that he accepted and held for thirty-four years, until his death.

During his long tenure (the longest of any U.S. chief justice), Marshall played a major role in developing America's legal system and in establishing the balance of power between the executive, legislative, and judicial branches of government. His groundbreaking decisions, which helped to strengthen the Constitution, continue to guide the Supreme Court today.

After a long and distinguished career that was devoted to public service, Marshall died in his Richmond home in 1835, at the age of seventy-nine. The house remained in the Marshall family until 1911, when it was sold to the City of Richmond. In 1913, the city conveyed stewardship of the house to the Association for the Preservation of Virginia Antiquities (now APVA Preservation Virginia), which opened it to the public. The city transferred ownership to the APVA in 2005. The house, which contains a large collection of Marshall family furnishings and memorabilia, was completely restored by APVA in 1976. It is open Tuesday through Sunday all year.

Designed in the 1970s, a backyard garden holds a variety of Marshall-era plants that bloom from spring through fall. In addition to flowerbeds that hold bulbs, perennials, and wildflowers, there is also an herb garden that consists of four parterres.

LEFT: *Identified as the large dining room, this multifunctional room served as the primary public space in the mansion and is decorated with fine neoclassical woodwork. Many social events were held in this room, including Marshall's monthly Sunday afternoon lawyers' dinners, which drew as many as thirty guests. The portrait above the fireplace, painted by William James Hubard, depicts Marshall at nearly eighty years of age.*

ABOVE: *The parlor, or withdrawing room, is elegantly styled with raised paneling and a classical fireplace mantel. To the right of the fireplace is a built-in cupboard; to the left is an arched entryway that accesses a passage and the small dining room.*

RIGHT: *In the Marshalls' large dining room, a lamp sits on the mahogany bookcase that was a wedding gift to the couple from Mary's parents. The bookcase held the chief justice's enormous collection of books.*

FACING PAGE: *In the backyard garden at the John Marshall House, a wooden chair beckons visitors to relax for a while. The intimate Marshall-era garden holds a selection of wildflowers, perennials, and herbs.*

Maymont

During the post–Civil War years of the late nineteenth century, an era known as the Gilded Age, financiers and industrialists such as John D. Rockefeller, J. P. Morgan, and Cornelius Vanderbilt amassed huge fortunes, which they spent lavishly. The most extravagant displays of their wealth and prosperity were the massive and elaborate mansions that they built.

In 1886, Major James Dooley, a Richmond-born financier and railroad magnate of that era, and his wife, Sallie, acquired 100 acres of dairy farmland on the banks of the James River in what was then Henrico County. They engaged architect Edgerton Rogers to design an opulent mansion, which would be the most elaborate in Richmond of that day. Completed in 1893, Rogers' creation is a thirty-three room, 12,000-square foot dwelling in the Romanesque Revival style, with elements of Queen Anne. The Dooleys named their Victorian estate Maymont, a combination of Mrs. Dooley's maiden name, May, and the Italian word for hill, *mont*.

The sturdy sandstone mansion has three floors, plus a full basement. Twelve rooms on the first and second floors are open for tours. The main rooms on the upper floors are located off of a large central hall, which holds the grand staircase. Above the stairs, a magnificent Tiffany Studios stained glass window allows light to pour into the second floor's central hall.

The house is delightfully eclectic, with each of its main rooms imparting a different feel and theme. This is accomplished by the blending of colors, textures, patterns, and historical styles that range from French eighteenth century to English Renaissance. Opulence and exceptional workmanship abound, from the drawing rooms with their gold-leafed mantels, white onyx hearthstones, silk damask wall coverings and ornamental plasterwork to the library with its ceiling and frieze adorned with intricate stenciling and rich mahogany strapwork.

Upon their deaths, the Dooleys, who were childless, bequeathed their Maymont estate—including its extraordinary collection of furnishings, antiques, and art—to the City of Richmond for use as a public park and museum. Maymont opened to the public six months after Mrs. Dooley's death in 1925, and the mansion's interiors were left mainly as they were until 1970, when a restoration began. It stands today remarkably intact and well preserved, and is recognized by the National Register of Historic Places as "a significant example of an American country estate of the Gilded Age." The private, nonprofit Maymont Foundation was formed in 1975 to manage the property.

Since luxurious landscapes were just as important to the Gilded Age millionaires as their elaborate mansions, the Dooleys spared no expense to develop their estate's diverse grounds, which include high bluffs, streams, ravines, and rock outcroppings. Aided by her estate manager and large groundskeeping staff, Mrs. Dooley, who was a passionate student of horticulture, directed the planting and care of her spectacular gardens. Today, Maymont's beautiful grounds and gardens are a glorious oasis in the middle of urban Richmond, perfect for leisurely strolls, family picnics, or quiet reflection.

As eclectic as the house, Maymont's landscaping encompasses a variety of themes. The extensive acreage of the estate is landscaped as English-style parkland, with lush grassy lawns and an arboretum that includes native Virginia trees and shrubs as well as more than two hundred exotic species. A classical, terraced Italian garden includes a wisteria-covered pergola, marvelous stonework, statuary, gazebos, fountains, and geometrically shaped flower beds. In contrast to its formality, a Japanese garden is more naturalistic. Its soothing shades of green, brown, and gray reflect the colors of nature. A path meanders through the cool and shaded garden, crossing over bridges and past trained and pruned trees and shrubs as it follows a winding watercourse down to a large pond, where water irises and water lilies bloom. In addition to these two large garden spaces, there are many other specialty gardens such as butterfly, daylily, and cactus gardens.

Several original outbuildings remain, including a carriage house that holds a large carriage collection. Other attractions, such as a nature center, wildlife exhibits, and a children's farm, have been added over the years. Maymont's grounds are open daily, while the indoor exhibits and house tours are offered Tuesday through Sunday.

FACING PAGE: *Like other magnificent mansions built during the Gilded Age, James and Sallie Dooley's Maymont was intended, at least in part, to be a lavish display of their wealth and status. Completed in 1893, the Romanesque-style sandstone mansion, with its towers, arches, and sumptuous interiors, was the nucleus of a 100-acre, lushly landscaped estate in Richmond.*

TOP: *Spring finds Maymont's formal terraced Italian Garden bedecked in red, white, and blue. Behind the flowerbeds, the garden's long pergola is draped with heavy clusters of lavender wisteria. The beds are replanted multiple times during the season, offering an ever-changing visual delight for Maymont's visitors.*

ABOVE: *Azaleas bloom around the pond in Maymont's enchanting Japanese garden. The original garden, which is believed to have been designed for the Dooleys by the master Japanese gardener Muto, was renovated and expanded in 1978. The current "stroll garden" contains pruned trees and shrubs, stone groupings, water areas, paths, bridges, and stone lanterns. The area is cool, shady, and serene—perfect for a leisurely stroll.*

RIGHT: *The library is perhaps the most eclectic room in the mansion. Rich mahogany wood is used throughout the room, including the mantel, the Venetian blinds, and the Jacobean strapwork on the ceiling. Interesting furnishings include an Italian Renaissance chair with carved winged lions at its arms.*

FACING PAGE, TOP: *The Dooleys held many elaborate dinner parties in their elegant dining room, which boasts rich quarter-sawn oak wainscoting. Food prepared by staff in the mansion's basement kitchen was sent up via dumbwaiter to servants in the butler's pantry, located just outside of the dining room.*

FACING PAGE, BOTTOM: *The most opulent room in the mansion is the pink drawing room, where Mrs. Dooley entertained her friends. The French-style room is extravagantly decorated, from its beautifully painted and plastered rococo-style ceiling and silk damask-covered walls to the woodwork made from imported South American primavera wood and the 14K-gold-plated chandelier and gold-leafed mantel.*

Scotchtown

16120 CHISWELL LANE
BEAVERDAM, VA 23015

"I know not what course others may take; but as for me, give me liberty or give me death." In March of 1775, Patrick Henry, a delegate from Hanover County, made his way to the Second Virginia Convention in Richmond from his home at Scotchtown, a tobacco plantation some 15 miles to the north. At the convention, he delivered the famous fiery speech that helped propel the colonies toward war with England and would forever brand him as a symbol of America's fight for freedom.

Although Patrick Henry was Scotchtown's most famous resident, he was not its first. In July of 1717, Charles Chiswell received 9,976 acres in a land grant from Lt. Governor Alexander Spotswood, and about two years later, he built a modest house. After Chiswell's death in 1737, his son, Col. John Chiswell, lived there with his family until about 1753. Evidence suggests that it was during Col. Chiswell's occupancy that the dwelling attained its present size. By 1760, Col. Chiswell had transferred ownership to his son-in-law, John Robinson, although it appears that Robinson never lived there. When Robinson died in 1766, Scotchtown was put up for sale to help pay off large debts that he owed to the state. It finally sold in 1770 to an unnamed buyer.

It is believed that Patrick Henry was the 1770 purchaser, though he did not make the final payment for the house and 960 acres until 1772. He and his pregnant wife, Sarah, and their five children most likely moved into the house in the spring of 1771. Shortly after giving birth to their sixth child, Sarah began to suffer from severe mental illness. Rather than commit her to the public mental hospital in Williamsburg, Henry chose to keep her at home where family could care for her. Before she died in 1775, she is believed to have spent her last years confined in chambers on the property.

In 1776, Henry was elected as Virginia's first governor, an office he would hold a total of five terms during his lifetime. After he married Dorothea Dandridge in 1777, the couple moved into the Governor's Palace in Williamsburg, and Henry put the plantation up for sale.

Little is known about Scotchtown between 1778 and 1801, during which time there were two owners. John Mosby Sheppard purchased it in 1801, and it remained in his family until 1958, at which time only 99 acres remained with the house. Records show that much remodeling was done to the house during the mid-nineteenth century. In 1958, the Association for the Preservation of Virginia Antiquities (now APVA Preservation Virginia) acquired Scotchtown at auction. The Association's Hanover County branch oversaw an extensive restoration that returned the house to its late-eighteenth-century appearance. Now operated by APVA's Headquarters in Richmond, the site is open for tours April through October

Scotchtown is a colonial-style, one-story, frame dwelling with eight large rooms and a large central passage that runs the length of the house and has doors at each end. The rooms are interpreted as the Henry family's east and west parlors, formal and informal dining rooms, a storage room, and three bedrooms. There is a full attic that contains a single large, unfinished room. According to a Henry descendant, that room was used for storage and play space as well as sleeping quarters for Henry's sons when visitors used their bedrooms. The rooms in the full basement were used by the Henrys for multiple purposes. Currently, they contain exhibits of agricultural tools and textile working equipment.

Several of Scotchtown's early-nineteenth-century outbuildings have been reconstructed, including an icehouse and kitchen. In the early 1970s, the Garden Club of Virginia oversaw landscaping at Scotchtown. The simple landscape is appropriate for what was, in the eighteenth century, an isolated, rural property. The grounds contain trees and boxwood that are believed to be original to the early nineteenth century.

FACING PAGE: *Scotchtown was the home of patriot and "voice of the Revolution" Patrick Henry, his wife, Sarah, and their six children. Henry purchased the house and 960-acre tobacco plantation in 1770 and made it his home from 1771 until 1778.*

ABOVE: *Located off of the central passage, the east parlor was most likely used as the Henry family's sitting room, where they would read, sew, and converse, or as a room for entertaining guests. The room contains fine raised-wood paneling and wainscoting. Above the fireplace hangs a portrait of George Washington painted by artist Charles Peale Polk.*

Montpelier

11407 CONSTITUTION HIGHWAY
MONTPELIER STATION, VA 22957

James Madison, one of the most influential of the nation's founding fathers, experienced a long and remarkable political career that included election to the Virginia Constitutional Convention, Virginia's General Assembly, the Virginia House of Delegates, and the Second Continental Congress. At the 1787 Constitutional Convention, his work as the chief architect of the new Constitution earned him the title "Father of the Constitution." He served two terms as secretary of state under President Jefferson, with whom he enjoyed a fifty-year friendship, and two terms as the fourth president of the United States.

Madison's lifetime home was Montpelier, the family plantation in Orange County, which his grandfather, Ambrose Madison, received by land grant in 1723. In 1765, Madison's father, James Madison Sr., built a two-story, brick, Georgian-style house with four rooms and a central passage on the first floor and five rooms on the second. That original structure makes up the core of the present mansion.

In 1794, Madison married Dolley Payne Todd, a widow with a two-year-old son, Payne. In 1797, Madison enlarged his father's house with a 30-foot addition to the northeast side that was laid out with a side-passage design, which gave it a duplex arrangement. It provided James and Dolley with a dining room and bedchamber downstairs and two bedchambers upstairs, which were separate from his parents' living quarters. He also added a large Tuscan portico on the front of the house.

In his next and final building phase, beginning in 1809, Madison added one-story wings (the cellars of which contained kitchens) on each side of the house. He renovated the interior, creating a small entry that opened into an elegant drawing room, and installed a fashionable Federal-style doorway with an oval fanlight above the door and glazed sidelights. A colonnade was added to the back of the house. Madison employed James Dinsmore and John Neilson, two of his friend Thomas Jefferson's master craftsmen from nearby Monticello, to work on the Montpelier expansion.

James Madison, the last surviving founding father, died at Montpelier in June 1836, at the age of eighty-five. By 1844, Dolley was forced to sell the estate to pay off debts. In the ensuing years, Montpelier had several owners and many alterations. After William duPont purchased it in 1901, he doubled its size (from twenty-two rooms to fifty-five rooms and twelve bathrooms) by raising the two wings to two stories, building two large additions onto the back, and adding a new kitchen wing. He left Montpelier to his daughter, Marion duPont Scott, an accomplished horsewoman who developed the estate into a prestigious horse training center.

Upon her death in 1983, Scott's heirs transferred Montpelier to the National Trust for Historic Preservation in accordance with her desire that they restore it to its Madison-era appearance. In 2000, the Montpelier Foundation was formed as a steward of Montpelier to administer the property for the National Trust. Opened to the public in 1987, Montpelier's mansion, grounds, gardens, and exhibits are now open year round.

In 2004, after intensive studies and architectural surveys had proven that carrying out an historically accurate restoration of the mansion to its circa-1820 appearance was feasible, teams of highly

FACING PAGE: *By 1812, James Madison had expanded his father's original circa-1765 nine-room house into a twenty-two-room mansion. Alterations made by subsequent owners, particularly the duPonts, greatly altered its appearance. A meticulous five-year restoration project has returned Montpelier to its Madison-era appearance.*

RIGHT: *Through the front doors of Montpelier, visitors enter a unique narrow vestibule with classical arched openings on all sides. Directly across from the front door is the drawing room, entered through double doors with glazed sidelights and an arched fanlight above. To the visitors' left at the end of the vestibule, an arched opening leads into James and Dolley's side of the house, while an arched opening to the right leads into his parents' quarters.*

trained historical restoration specialists went to work on returning Montpelier to the house that was lived in and loved by James Madison. By 2006, the exterior was completed, including the removal of all post-Madison additions and the pink stucco that a previous owner had applied to the original brick façade. The interior will be completed by autumn 2008. Based on the results of ongoing research, the mansion will eventually be furnished with original and period objects.

Montpelier's nearly 2,700 acres offer mountain vistas, rolling pastureland with grazing thoroughbreds, and the 200-year-old Landmark Forest. In the early 1800s, Madison had a 4-acre, horseshoe-shaped garden containing vegetables, flowers, fruit trees, and shrubs. Finding Madison's original garden sadly neglected, William duPont's wife, Annie, turned it into a 2-acre, early-twentieth-century formal garden with flowerbeds, shrubs, and trees. Marion duPont Scott later hired landscape architect Charles Gillette to design additional perennial beds. In 1990, the Garden Club of Virginia funded a restoration of the Annie duPont Formal Garden, which today aims to exemplify a typical early-1900s formal garden. Accessed by formal walkways, the sweeping garden is filled with crescent-shaped beds and parterres featuring an array of colorful perennials and annuals, along with boxwood and other shrubs.

LEFT: *Annie duPont transformed Montpelier's neglected garden into a 2-acre formal terraced garden with flower beds, shrubs, and trees. A May visit finds the restored early-1900s garden at its colorful peak, with purple irises and other perennials putting on a show.*

FACING PAGE, BOTTOM: *In the large upstairs bedchamber, a door beside the fireplace opens out onto a terrace, where family members and guests could socialize while enjoying views of the rolling pastureland and Blue Ridge Mountains beyond. The terrace was built on the roof deck of the north wing that was constructed in 1809.*

BELOW: *In the 1809–1812 construction phase, Madison demolished the wall that separated the two sides of the house and created a central drawing room that opens off of a vestibule. With its elegant arched doorway, classical overdoor pediment, ornate cornice, and tall triple-sashed windows, it is the most elaborate room in the mansion. The floors and most of the room's other woodwork are original to 1812.*

Monticello

ROUTE 53/THOMAS JEFFERSON
PARKWAY
CHARLOTTESVILLE, VA 22902

From the age of twenty-five until his "retirement" at age sixty-six, Thomas Jefferson devoted his life to his state and nation, serving in the House of Burgesses and the Continental Congress (where he authored the Declaration of Independence), and as governor of Virginia, minister to France, secretary of state, vice president, and, finally, president of the United States. Gifted with a brilliant mind, insatiable curiosity, and a myriad of interests and talents, Jefferson was a true "man of the Enlightenment" who, in addition to helping to create and run a new nation, was also a plantation owner, gardener, scientist, inventor, scholar, violinist, and author.

Jefferson was also a talented, self-taught architect, an avocation he found most gratifying. He studied numerous books on the subject, particularly the *Four Books of Architecture* by Renaissance Italian Andrea Palladio. He designed two houses for himself and consulted with many friends on their house plans. He also designed such public structures as the Virginia State Capitol building in Richmond and the magnificent rotunda and grounds of the University of Virginia, which he founded.

In 1769, Jefferson began construction on his beloved home, Monticello (Italian for "little mountain"). He built it on a small mountaintop near Charlottesville, part of a 5,000-acre tract of land inherited from his father. "Architecture is my delight," Jefferson said, "and putting up and pulling down, one of my favorite amusements." Monticello was certainly a testament to this statement, for he designed, built, modified, redesigned, tore down, and rebuilt the mansion over a forty-year period.

The first version, a brick, two-story home with eight rooms and a cellar, was nearly complete by 1784 when Jefferson left for Paris, where he served five years as minister to France. While there, he became increasingly enamored with European architecture. He returned to America in 1789, full of ideas for remodeling Monticello. Construction on his new designs began in 1796 and continued until 1809, resulting in the architectural masterpiece visitors see today.

The Roman neoclassical-style mansion contains twenty-one rooms on three floors, plus twelve rooms in the basement. Two L-shaped dependency wings containing service rooms and slave quarters extend from each side of the house. They are built on the level of the house's basement and positioned so as not to be visible from the main entrances. Their roofs, which are level with the house's main floor, serve as terrace walkways. Small pavilions stand at the end of each wing.

TOP: *The west front of Thomas Jefferson's Monticello is also known as the "nickel view," since it is pictured on the back of the U.S. nickel. Construction on the house began in 1769 but would not be completed in its present form until 1809. A flower-bordered serpentine walkway snakes around the perimeter of the oval-shaped west lawn.*

LEFT: *As is the case today, most of Jefferson's visitors would arrive at the mansion's east front and enter through the columned portico into the entrance hall. One of Jefferson's many innovations was a compass that he installed in the ceiling of the portico. The compass was connected to a weathervane on the roof, thus allowing him to determine the wind direction simply by looking out the window of the entrance hall.*

In creating Monticello, the only house in America on the United Nations' World Heritage List, Jefferson combined his love of classical architecture with his affinity for modern innovations. Consequently, in addition to its many classical elements, including elaborate friezes, graceful arches and fanlights, and a spectacular dome, the house also contains unique features that Jefferson, the pragmatist, added for the sake of function or convenience, such as thirteen skylights to maximize light, alcove beds to save space, and three indoor privies.

Jefferson lived at Monticello until his death on July 4, 1826, the fiftieth anniversary of the signing of the Declaration of Independence. Unfortunately, he died in debt, and his family was forced to sell Monticello. In 1834, Uriah P. Levy purchased the house, hoping to preserve it as a national monument. It remained in that family's care until 1923, when they sold it to the nonprofit Thomas Jefferson Foundation, which owns and operates Monticello today as a museum.

Along with the house and dependencies (open for tours daily), a visit to Monticello includes its magnificent flower, vegetable, and fruit gardens. In addition to providing food and ornamentation, these gardens served as botanical laboratories for Jefferson, who experimented with flowers and food plants from around the world.

Between 1939 and 1941, the Garden Club of Virginia undertook a restoration of Jefferson's flower gardens, which had all but disappeared after his death. They authentically restored the gardens using Jefferson's original design sketches from 1807 and his Garden Book, a detailed diary of the horticultural happenings at Monticello, including plant lists.

There are two main elements of Monticello's flower garden. The first consists of twenty oval-shaped beds placed immediately around the four corners of the house, each of which is planted with a different flower. The second element is a flower-bordered winding walkway that defines the perimeter of the expansive, oval-shaped west lawn. According to documentation, Jefferson's diverse plantings included some 105 species of annuals, perennials, biennials, and old rose varieties. Those

recorded by Jefferson make up the foundation of today's gardens.

In his 1,000-foot-long terraced vegetable garden, Jefferson grew over 250 varieties of different vegetable species. The current garden, which is based on documentation plus two years of archeological excavation, attempts to re-create Jefferson's garden as it looked between 1807 and 1814.

TOP: *Young spring vegetables grow in a portion of Jefferson's re-created 2-acre vegetable garden, while the hillside orchard below is abloom with the colorful blossoms of fruit trees and redbud.*

RIGHT: *Monticello's spacious entrance hall is seen from the balcony of the mezzanine level. Because the entrance hall was used as a reception area and waiting room for Jefferson's many visitors, he elected to treat it as a museum, filling it with art, busts of prominent figures, maps, Indian artifacts, and natural-history specimens. The decorative pattern on the ceiling of the 18-foot room features an eagle-and-stars design.*

FACING PAGE, TOP: *Jefferson had this attractive fishpond constructed on Monticello's west lawn so that he could enjoy fresh fish anytime. Fish were caught in the nearby river and streams, brought back to Monticello alive, and released into the pond, where they remained until they became the fresh fish of the day at the Jeffersons' dining table.*

ABOVE: *The octagonal-shaped tea room at Monticello is separated from the adjoining dining room by an elegant arched opening with double pocket doors on rollers. Jefferson used the tea room for reading and writing as well as dining, and in it he placed busts of friends and prominent figures, such as Benjamin Franklin, George Washington, and Lafayette.*

LEFT: *The parlor, with a gorgeous cherry and beech parquet floor designed by Jefferson, was used for large social functions as well as smaller family affairs. Furnishings include the campeachy or "siesta" chairs in front of the fireplace. The comfortable campeachy was Jefferson's favorite chair, especially as he began to suffer the infirmities of advancing years.*

BELOW: *In Jefferson's private suite of rooms, a partition wall with a bed alcove separates his bedchamber from his study. Above the bed is a closet, which he accessed by a steep stair or ladder. He added the three elliptical openings to provide the closet with light (which came from the chamber's skylight) and ventilation. One of the home's three indoor privies is also located in the room.*

Ash Lawn–Highland

1000 James Monroe Parkway
Charlottesville, VA 22902

Prior to serving two terms as America's fifth president (1817–1825), James Monroe had already distinguished himself as a man devoted to his state and country. In 1776, eighteen-year-old Monroe left his studies at the College of William & Mary to fight alongside George Washington during the Revolutionary War. He was severely wounded and cited for bravery during the Battle of Trenton. After the revolution, he went on to hold more public offices than any other president, including U.S. senator, minister to France, Spain, and England, governor of Virginia, secretary of state, secretary of war, and, finally, president.

When Monroe returned to Virginia after the Revolutionary War, he studied law under Thomas Jefferson, who became his close friend and mentor. Encouraged by Jefferson, Monroe, with his wife, Elizabeth, moved to Albemarle County in 1789. They owned a house in Charlottesville as well as an 800-acre farm, which included a house and office, located at the site of the current University of Virginia. In 1793, Monroe purchased 1,500 acres of farmland that adjoined Jefferson's Monticello. This acreage eventually increased to 3,500 acres.

President George Washington sent Monroe to serve as secretary to France from 1794 to 1797. When he returned to Virginia, he began construction on a new house on his Albemarle County plantation, which he named Highland. The Monroes settled in at Highland in late 1799, and it remained their official residence for twenty-four years.

The house, which Monroe referred to as his "cabin castle," was a simple, one-story, frame farmhouse with a wing, quite modest indeed when compared to Jefferson's Monticello. Over the years,

further improvements were made to the house, including the addition of another wing. The Monroes also added a stone kitchen cellar, an uncommon feature for homes of this time period, which normally had detached kitchens. The idea may have come from Jefferson, who also had a basement kitchen at Monticello.

After they built a new mansion in Loudoun County, the Monroes sold Highland in 1826. It had numerous owners over the years, one of whom, Alexander Garrett, changed the name to Ash Lawn. Today, both names are used. In 1882, a later owner, John Massey, built a two-story addition on top of the foundation of Monroe's original east wing, which had burned earlier in the century.

Philanthropist Jay Winston Johns purchased the property in 1930 and soon opened it for public tours. When he died in 1974, he willed it to the College of William & Mary, Monroe's alma mater, stipulating that it be managed "as a historic shrine for the education of the general public." Today, the college operates the 535-acre property as a working farm, house museum, and performing arts site. It is open year round.

The house tour begins in the entrance hall and exhibition room, located in the two-story addition that was built by Massey. From there, visitors step down into the original level of the Monroe house, which includes the drawing room, dining room, master bedchamber, children's bedchamber, and study. Ninety percent of the house's furnishings are Monroe pieces, including such interesting items as the bust of Napoleon that was given to Monroe by Napoleon himself, in recognition of his negotiations for the Louisiana Purchase. Some of these pieces are on loan. A few are meticulously crafted reproductions of Monroe items, while others are "twins" to known Monroe pieces.

Outside, plantation buildings, including an original 1800 smoke house, a reconstructed slave and guest quarters, and a restored 1818 plantation office, are located in the service yard. Inside a century-old English and American boxwood garden, a large white oak tree from Monroe's day still proudly stands. Ornamental and utilitarian gardens hold typical 1800s plantings that would have provided fresh and dried flowers for bouquets, and herbs for cooking, scenting, dyeing, and medicinal purposes. A vegetable garden is planted in peas, beans, corn, squash, and tomatoes.

Cattle, sheep, chickens, and even some peacocks complete Monroe's serenely beautiful farm, set in the foothills of the Blue Ridge Mountains.

FACING PAGE: *Built in 1799, Highland was the official residence of James Monroe for twenty-four years, including the period of his two terms as president (1817–1825). The front door of Monroe's "cabin castle" opens into a formal garden. The two-story portion of the house was added in 1882 by a later owner. Original and reconstructed plantation outbuildings stand in the service yard behind the house.*

ABOVE: *Prominently displayed in the Monroes' drawing room is the Chaudet bust of Napoleon that was given to Monroe by Napoleon himself in recognition of his negotiations for the Louisiana Purchase. The English pianoforte is like the one owned by the Monroes and played by one of their daughters, Maria Hester.*

ABOVE: *The scholarly and hard-working Monroe spent much of his time in his study at Highland, where he kept a large personal library. The secretary in this room is believed to be a Monroe family piece. Portraits on the walls include friends and members of his cabinet.*

RIGHT: *The dining room was used for entertaining as well as family meals. The Monroes purchased the Hepplewhite mahogany dining table shortly after they were married in 1786. They used the Federal-style chairs while at the White House.*

ABOVE: *Most of the furnishings in the master bedchamber are original pieces owned by the Monroes. The mahogany bed features high posts that are hand carved with a feather-and-palm design. The late-eighteenth-century crib was most likely used by the Monroe children. The marble-topped washstand was made in Washington, D.C., during Monroe's presidency.*

LEFT: *Ash Lawn–Highland's vegetable garden is enclosed by a white picket fence. Flowers planted along the fence line are both ornamental and utilitarian. The pretty red bee balm, also called bergamot or Oswego tea, was used as a balm for bee stings. The leaves could be used to soothe nerves or an upset stomach.*

Point of Honor

112 CABELL STREET
LYNCHBURG, VA 24504

Dr. George Cabell was a prominent Lynchburg physician whose most famous patient was Patrick Henry. As his physician and also his friend, Dr. Cabell was called to Red Hill Plantation in June of 1799 to provide medical treatment during Henry's last illness. Cabell also maintained a friendship with Thomas Jefferson, whose Poplar Forest plantation was located nearby.

In 1805, Cabell purchased 856 acres of land along the James River at Lynchburg, where he built and operated a tobacco warehouse. Along with his wife, Sarah, and their eight children, he resided many years in a fine house in town before he decided to build a much grander home on his James River property. Completed around 1815, Cabell's new home, which sat on a hilltop overlooking the river, came to be known as Point of Honor, a name inspired by tales of duels that were reportedly fought on the property.

Point of Honor is a stylish, two-story, Federal-style mansion with an English basement. It is constructed of brick laid in Flemish bond and has a shallow hipped roof covered with oak shingles. Rather than a plain flat front, which is characteristic of most Federal Piedmont dwellings, Point of Honor boasts two semi-octagon bays on each side of the entrance that give it a striking appearance. Adding to the appeal are doorways crowned with arched fanlights. Inside, rooms on the first floor—a parlor, dining room, and main bedchamber—are located off of a wide entry hall. The hall contains a stairway that accesses four additional bedrooms on the second floor.

Point of Honor is noted for its excellent interior woodwork, like the carved pineapple design located on the mantel and overdoor pediment in the parlor. The carvings were based on designs from the late-eighteenth- and early-nineteenth-century books of Owen Biddle and William Pain, which offered ideas on decorating trends of that day.

After George Cabell died in 1823, his son, William, inherited the property. It passed out of the Cabell family in 1830, when twenty-four-year-old William and his wife, Eliza, both died of tuberculosis, leaving Point of Honor to Eliza's father, Judge William Daniel. Over the next century, several more distinguished Lynchburg families made this remarkable house their home.

In 1928, James R. Gilliam Jr. purchased the property and donated it to the city of Lynchburg. It then served as a soup kitchen during the Depression, a nursery for working women during World War II, and a community center. In 1968, the city deeded the house to the Lynchburg Historical Foundation.

In 1971, a retired schoolteacher, Katharine Garland Diggs, left a bequest to establish a city museum in Lynchburg, and Point of Honor was chosen as its location. In 1976–77, the house was carefully restored back to the Cabell era through the joint efforts of the Lynchburg Historical Foundation, the Diggs Trust, and the City of Lynchburg. It has been appropriately furnished with period pieces. The historic house museum, which opened to the public in 1978, is owned and administered by Point of Honor Inc., a charitable nonprofit foundation, in partnership with the Lynchburg Museum System. It is open daily, all year.

The Garden Club of Virginia restored the front grounds of Point of Honor in the late 1970s. The club designed a circular drive with stones and cobblestones that leads up to the front of the house. English boxwood were planted along the front and drive circle. Later, the club designed a plan for perennial beds in the rear of the house and provided trees and shrubs to landscape the parking area. The Garden Club also provided the landscaping around a carriage house and a re-created kitchen built in the 1990s.

ABOVE: *Home of prominent Lynchburg surgeon Dr. George Cabell, Point of Honor is an elegant Federal-style mansion built circa 1815. It is most noted for its two matching semi-octagonal bays that flank the main entrance, as well as for its exceptional interior woodwork.*

LEFT: *The fashionable parlor is where the Cabell family entertained their guests. The room is full of vivid colors, typical of the Federal era. The stylish wallpaper is a reproduction of Dufour's "Monuments of Paris," published in France in 1814. The carpeting, which was not typical in most Piedmont Federal homes, is Brussels weave, re-created from an English pattern book of 1800.*

Poplar Forest

Weary from his many years of public service, Thomas Jefferson longed for a tranquil retreat away from the public eye where he could relax and pursue his many interests. Not even his beloved Monticello could afford him that luxury, since there was a constant stream of visitors coming to see him there.

Jefferson designed a house for himself to be built at Poplar Forest, a 4,819-acre working plantation that he owned in Bedford County, near Lynchburg. Construction began in 1806, during his second presidential term. The inspiration for his home came from the classical idea of a Roman villa retreat: a country home designed for relaxation and pleasure. The renowned Renaissance architect Andrea Palladio, whom Jefferson studied and admired, had written, "The ancient sages commonly used to retire to such places."

At this, his private retreat, Jefferson felt free to follow his "fancy" with its design. Using elements of ancient, Renaissance Palladian, and eighteenth-century French architecture, along with British and Virginian designs, he blended together countless ideas and designs that appealed to him to create a dwelling that was uniquely Jefferson.

Influenced by his years in Paris, where he noted that "all the new and good houses" were one story, Jefferson built his house into the crown of a hill so that the two-story structure appeared to be one story from the front. The main level contained the living area, and the lower level held a wine cellar and service and storage areas. Other French touches included a skylight, floor-to-ceiling windows,

an indoor privy, and alcove beds, features he had also added at Monticello.

Following the predilections of his mathematical mind, Jefferson designed his house as a perfect, equal-sided octagon. Its interior is divided into four elongated octagons, which were used as bedchambers, a parlor, and storage. They surround a central room that is a perfect cube. The cube room, measuring 20 feet in all directions, was the heart of Jefferson's house, used for dining and other gatherings, and connected to the rest of the house by glass doors that allowed for the passage of air and light. With no exterior walls, this soaring, two-story room is lit from above by a magnificent 16-foot sky-

light. After construction began, for reasons of practicality, he added two porticos, two stair pavilions, and six doorways, even though these additions altered the geometry of the perfect octagon.

Jefferson was occupying the house by 1809, and he slowly completed the house over the next seventeen years. By 1812, craftsmen had finished the main house, which boasted fine European-style oak floors and classical entablatures with ornamental frieze elements. In 1814, a 100-foot-long service wing was added to the east side.

When Jefferson died in 1826, he left Poplar Forest to his grandson, Francis Eppes. Eppes sold it in 1828, and subsequent owners made renovations that severely altered Jefferson's original design. All but 50 acres of the plantation were sold off over time, and subdivisions soon crowded around it.

In 1984, a group of local citizens, dedicated to saving the historic but deteriorating property, formed the nonprofit Corporation for Thomas Jefferson's Poplar Forest to lead an initiative to rescue Jefferson's retreat home and curtilage acreage. Poplar Forest was opened for public visitation in 1986, and its rescue and restoration continue today.

In 1993, after intensive archaeological investigation and research, which included the study of some fifteen hundred of Jefferson's letters relating to Poplar Forest, restoration began. Skilled crews are using the same building methods as Jefferson's craftsmen and replicating their materials as closely as possible, right down to the hand-molded bricks and authentically re-created mortar and plaster. Exterior restorations on the main house were completed in 1998. Using Jefferson's detailed letters as their guide, today's craftsmen continue the interior finish work in the same sequence as Jefferson's own workers. Work also continues on the rebuilding of the east service wing, which had been removed by a previous owner. Restoration of Jefferson's landscaping will follow.

Visitors to Poplar Forest (open Wednesday–Monday from April through November) can witness this remarkable restoration in progress. Many return regularly, eager to watch the transformation as Jefferson's masterpiece is returned to its original grandeur.

FACING PAGE: *In 1806, Thomas Jefferson began construction of a house at his Poplar Forest plantation, which he intended as a private country retreat. By 1809, he was in residence at the octagonal home, but work continued for seventeen more years. Striking details of the home's exterior include the classical balustrade and Chinese rail atop the roof and a pedimented portico with fanlight.*

ABOVE: *The south-facing room in the house is the parlor, seen here during restoration. Jefferson did much of his reading in this room, which is filled with light from the floor-to-ceiling windows, an idea he adopted from the French architecture he so admired. When the bottom portions of the triple-sash windows are raised, the openings serve as doorways to the portico.*

Prestwould Plantation

U.S. ROUTE 15
CLARKSVILLE, VA 23927

Perched on a bluff high above the Roanoke River in far Southside Virginia, Prestwould Plantation, with its handsome manor house and original outbuildings, was once the center of a thriving 10,000-acre plantation owned by Sir Peyton Skipwith, an American-born baronet. When it was built, Prestwould, named after Sir Peyton's ancestral home in England, was one of the largest gentry houses in Virginia.

Sir Peyton and his second wife, Lady Jean Skipwith, completed Prestwould in about 1795. The massive, two-story, late-Georgian, early-Federal-style mansion has a hipped roof and an English basement and is constructed of stone that was quarried on the plantation. The first floor contains a dining room, a parlor, a drawing room, and Sir Peyton's bedchamber, all located off of a wide central hallway. The hallway itself is divided into two separate rooms, an entrance hall and a saloon, a layout modeled after the grand manor houses in England. The second floor holds four additional bedrooms.

After Sir Peyton's death in 1805, Lady Jean managed the plantation until her own death in 1826. It prospered under her capable management, and she went on to become one of the nation's wealthiest women. Lady Jean's oldest son, Humberston, a widower, took possession of Prestwould after her death. Two years later, he married his widowed cousin, Lelia Skipwith Robertson, and they subsequently redecorated Prestwould in the neoclassical style that was popular at that time.

A total of four generations of Skipwiths lived at Prestwould before it was sold out of the family in 1914. It then changed hands five times before the Roanoke River Museum (now the nonprofit

Prestwould Foundation) acquired the vacant and deteriorating property in 1963 and undertook its meticulous restoration.

The house stands today remarkably unaltered and retains most of its original yellow pine floors, doors, and fine regional Georgian woodwork. It is well noted for the survival of its late-eighteenth-century English botanical wallpapers and its French scenic wallpapers from the early nineteenth century. Many Skipwith family furnishings, including fine English furniture that was purchased when the house was built and neoclassical furniture from the second generation of Skipwiths, have been returned to the site and, with the help of old photographs and documents, have been placed in their original locations in the house. This allows visitors the opportunity to view the house very much the way it looked during the Skipwiths' occupancies. The hall, parlor, and Sir Peyton's chamber are interpreted to Lady Jean's era, while the dining room, drawing room, and saloon reflect the era of Lelia Skipwith.

Also notable at Prestwould is the survival of more than ten thousand documents relating to the plantation, including letters, diaries, and detailed invoices, as well as one of the nation's largest collections of slave writings, which detail plantation life from a slave's perspective. These documents have been invaluable to the foundation during its restoration efforts.

In 1980, the Garden Club of Virginia undertook an interpretive restoration of Lady Jean's extensive garden and, over the years, donated an irrigation system and garden gates. An avid plant collector and experimenter, Lady Jean kept detailed records, making her garden one of the best documented of that era. The original plan consisted of a grid of walkways with garden beds in between and a long border of horseshoe-shaped beds on the west side. Her plantings included flowers, roses, and ornamental shrubs, as well as vegetables, herbs, berries, and fruit trees. Her octagonal summerhouse still anchors the garden's south end. The monumental task of returning Lady Jean's garden to its original grandeur is a project that will progress as funds become available.

Restoration and preservation work is ongoing on the mansion as well as the original plantation outbuildings, which include a plantation store, a loom house, an office, a summer house, smokehouses, and an early two-family slave house. The combination of the magnificently preserved manor house with its original furnishings, the original plantation outbuildings, and the existing documentation on the lives of the people who lived and worked there makes Prestwould one of the most complete plantations surviving in the South. The property is open for tours from April through October.

FACING PAGE: *Sir Peyton Skipwith and his second wife, Lady Jane, built this late-Georgian/early-Federal-style stone mansion on their 10,000-acre Prestwould Plantation in about 1795, and it was the seat of the Skipwith family for four generations.*

RIGHT: *Modeled after the grand manor houses of England, the large center hall at Prestwould is divided into two separate large rooms. The Hall, on the land side, was the business entrance. The riverside entrance, seen here, is called the Saloon. It was the entrance for personal and social uses and, as such, was elegantly decorated. Original early-nineteenth-century French scenic wallpaper, "Le Parc Français," hangs on the far wall.*

Part IV

WEST OF THE BLUE RIDGE

Long Branch

830 Long Branch Lane
(Routes 624 and 626)
Millwood, VA 22646

In 1798, Robert Carter Burwell, the great-great-grandson of wealthy Tidewater planter Robert "King" Carter, inherited 1,000 acres of rolling farmland in the northern Shenandoah Valley. It had been part of an original 50,212-acre tract that had been divided among "King" Carter's sons and grandsons in 1740.

Still a minor when he moved to present-day Clarke County, Burwell lived with his sister, Sarah, and her husband, Philip Nelson. Nelson moved to the valley in the late 1790s to help Nathaniel Burwell (great-uncle of Sarah and Robert) of nearby Carter Hall plantation establish a mill and mercantile in Millwood. He purchased land adjacent to Robert Burwell's, and they ran the properties together as one large wheat plantation.

Once he reached adulthood, Burwell planned a grand home of his own, soliciting advice on its design from Benjamin Henry Latrobe, a renowned architect of the U.S. Capitol. The site he chose for the house, along a stream known as Long Branch, was at the top of a rise that afforded him spectacular views of the bucolic countryside and Blue Ridge Mountains. Construction began on the impressive hipped-roofed Georgian-style mansion around 1811. Built of brick laid in Flemish bond, the two-story home with full basement featured an expansive central hallway on each floor, flanked by two large rooms on either side—a typical Georgian floor plan.

The house was still unfinished in 1813 when Burwell left to fight in the War of 1812. He became ill and died that same year, leaving Long Branch to Sarah and Philip, who lived there for a number of years, running the wheat plantation with their nine children. For a time, the Nelsons' daughters also ran a girls' school there. In 1842, Philip sold Long Branch to his nephew Major Hugh Mortimer Nelson, who along with his wife, Adelaide, dramatically changed the mansion's appearance by making numerous expansions and renovations that reflected the popular Greek Revival style.

In the grand hallway, the Nelsons built a magnificent spiral staircase, which spans three floors. Above the sweeping arc of the staircase, light streams down into the house through a belvedere that was constructed on the roof, enhancing the dramatic effect. Elaborately carved Greek Revival woodwork, based on designs by prominent architect Minard Lafever, was added in the hallway and parlors. What had previously been an east-wing loggia (open-sided room) was enclosed to create more living space. The addition of elegant columned porticos gave the mansion's exterior a more grand appearance, as did a widow's walk and the belvedere.

Hugh Nelson died of typhoid in 1862 while serving in the Confederate army, leaving Adelaide with large debts that he had accrued against Long Branch. She and her son, Hugh Jr., fought through years of court battles to hold onto the property, which remained in the Nelson family until 1957.

After languishing under three different owners, the deteriorating property was purchased at public auction in 1986 by eighty-three-year-old Harry Z. Isaacs, a wealthy Baltimore textile executive. Over a three-year period, he meticulously restored and renovated the house and added a west wing for balance. Isaacs furnished the thirteen-room mansion with exquisite period pieces and fabrics, which he collected during his frequent travels throughout Europe and the United States.

Soon after purchasing Long Branch, Isaacs learned that he had terminal cancer. Before his death in 1990, he established the nonprofit Harry Z. Isaacs Foundation to preserve and manage his historic estate "for the enjoyment and education of the American people." Today, the beautiful grounds of the 400-acre working farm in Virginia hunt country are open to the public daily throughout the year. House tours are available Wednesday through Sunday in spring, summer, and fall.

In 1997, Long Branch's Sheila Macqueen Gardens were dedicated to that renowned British floral arranger. The various ornamental areas feature herbs, hellebores, hostas, roses, perennials, and other plantings that Macqueen loved to use in her own English gardens. The gardens are maintained by the Sheila Macqueen Flower Ladies.

TOP: *Robert Carter Burwell began building a brick Georgian manor house at his Long Branch Plantation in 1811, but he died before it was finished. In the mid-nineteenth century, owners Hugh and Adelaide Nelson expanded and renovated the mansion in the Greek Revival style. The west wing was added in 1987 by Long Branch's last private owner, Harry Z. Isaacs.*

RIGHT: *The Sheila Macqueen Gardens beautify the grounds of Long Branch. The gardens are made up of individual ornamental areas that showcase different plantings that Macqueen, a celebrated British floral designer, used in her own gardens. They include assortments of perennials, roses, hostas, and hellebores, attractively displayed throughout the grounds.*

FACING PAGE: *Hugh and Adelaide Nelson built a spectacular spiral staircase in Long Branch's entrance hall. The graceful sweeping stairway, along with the two intricately carved columns, creates a dramatic entrance to the mansion. The staircase spans all three levels, and light streams down from the belvedere on the mansion's roof.*

ABOVE: *The elaborate carved woodwork above the doors and windows of the north and south parlors was added during renovations made by the Nelsons. The carvings are based on designs in an 1835 builder's pattern book published by renowned architect Minard Lafever.*

RIGHT: *Harry Z. Isaac's passion for horses led him to develop the property's*

400 acres into a working horse farm. His love of horses and dogs is evident in the Hunt Room and throughout the mansion in myriad paintings and sculptures. He also filled the house with a fabulous collection of eighteenth- and nineteenth-century furnishings acquired during his extensive travels.

Abram's Delight

1340 SOUTH PLEASANT
VALLEY ROAD
WINCHESTER, VA 22601

When Abraham Hollingsworth first arrived in present-day Winchester around 1728, the Shenandoah Valley was still very much Virginia's western frontier, with few colonial settlers. The grandson of Valentine Hollingsworth, a Quaker who had migrated to America from Ireland in 1682, Abraham came to the valley looking for the perfect location to establish a mill and build a home for his family, who were waiting back in Maryland.

Abraham received a grant of 582 acres of land in a beautiful area that he described as a "delight to behold." Other sources tell a different version, stating that, in his search for suitable land, Abraham came across a group of Shawnee Indians camped beside a plentiful spring. He quickly laid claim to 582 acres, for which he paid the Indians a cow, a calf, and a piece of red cloth. In fact, both accounts are likely true, for the Shawnees, believing the land to be rightfully theirs, may not have recognized Abraham's claim of ownership and may well have insisted on payment for themselves.

Abraham brought his family from Maryland and built a log house and a gristmill beside the spring—the beginnings of what would become a thriving center of industry and hospitality in the years to follow. After Abraham's death in 1748, his son, Isaac, inherited the property. In 1754, he constructed a fine stone house to replace the log cabin and named it Abram's Delight, in honor of his father. Isaac's house was considered a mansion compared to those of his neighbors, which were still mostly simple log structures. Built by Simon Taylor, a skilled stonemason, the house boasted

110 | VIRGINIA'S HISTORIC HOMES & GARDENS

22-inch walls made of native blue-gray limestone and a gable roof with interior stone chimneys at each end. The original two-story, three-bay dwelling featured a two-over-two floor plan with a central passage, a plan that was popular with Scotch-Irish settlers during this period. Since Isaac also intended to use his home as a Quaker meetinghouse, he had a moveable wall installed in the dining room. The hinged wall could be raised and fastened to hooks on the opposite wall, thus providing room for large gatherings.

In 1800, after Isaac's son Jonah had inherited the property, he built a two-story west wing addition to accommodate his large family. Dormer windows added to the roof allowed the house's attic to be used as a large sleeping loft for his thirteen children. The windows were removed during a later remodeling.

Jonah's son, David, who acquired Abram's Delight in 1830, made many changes and improvements. The moveable wall was made permanent, and the stairway was moved from the northwest corner of the dining room to its current position in the center hallway. Greek Revival trim replaced the original woodwork. Outside, he rebuilt the mill and constructed a large lake on the south side of the house.

David's three children, who never married, inherited the property prior to the Civil War. After Jonah Isaac and Mary died, Annie remained there alone. In her seventies, after arranging to leave it to two cousins who agreed to care for her for the rest of her life, Annie vacated the house, leaving it unoccupied (except for the ghosts that reportedly roam the halls) for nearly thirty years.

In 1943, the City of Winchester purchased the historic but sadly deteriorated property from the Hollingsworth cousins in order to preserve the city's oldest house and the home of one of its most prominent families. The Winchester–Frederick County Historical Society worked for nine years to restore the house, which is filled with many original family pieces.

Behind the house is a small perennial garden. The old gristmill serves as a gift shop and exhibit space. Also on the property is a log cabin similar to the one Abraham built in 1735. Built around 1780, the cabin, which originally stood in downtown Winchester, was dismantled and moved to Abram's Delight in the 1960s.

The historic house is open for tours April through October.

FACING PAGE: *Built by Isaac Hollingsworth in 1754, Abram's Delight is the oldest house in Winchester. The handsome two-story residence, built of native limestone, also served as the area's first Quaker meetinghouse. Members of the Hollingsworth family were the only people to ever live in the home, which was purchased by the City of Winchester in 1945.*

RIGHT: *The stylish parlor at Abram's Delight, along with the rest of the house, is furnished with fine eighteenth- and nineteenth-century antiques and Hollingsworth family heirlooms.*

Glen Burnie

901 AMHERST STREET
WINCHESTER, VA 22601

In 1735, surveyor James Wood received a grant for 1,200 acres of land in the beautiful northern Shenandoah Valley. A few years later, he and his wife, Mary, built a house and began farming on the fertile land. In 1744, Wood donated a portion of his land to form a settlement, called Frederick Town. Later renamed Winchester, it was the first English-speaking town west of the Blue Ridge.

Wood, who held the position of Clerk of Court, was one of Winchester's most prominent residents. He also had many influential friends, one of whom was George Washington. As a young surveyor for Lord Fairfax, Washington frequented Winchester, and as commander of the Virginia Regiment during the French and Indian War, Colonel Washington chose Winchester as the location for Fort Loudoun, his regimental headquarters. With Wood's assistance, Washington won his first public election in 1758 and became a member of the House of Burgesses.

James Wood's son, Robert, inherited the property, called Glen Burnie, in 1794 and began construction of his own dwelling. Built in two phases, from 1794 to 1797, the structure was a typical "I-house"—a dwelling that was normally two full stories and featured a central hallway with one room on each side. This original structure remains as the central core of today's Glen Burnie Historic House.

In 1884, with no other Wood namesakes to inherit it, Glen Burnie passed to William Wood Glass, son of Kitty Wood and Thomas Glass, and it thereafter remained in the Glass family. In 1955, Julian Wood Glass Jr. became the last family member to own the home, which he kept as a country retreat.

Once he took possession, Glass immediately began the transformation of Glen Burnie into the exquisite showplace visitors see today. He began by removing and replacing the deteriorated north

and south wings, which had been added to the Georgian-style house in the 1800s. The first level of the new south wing was designed as a drawing room, while the north wing featured a breakfast room and kitchen. Although he turned the dining room of the original house into his library and made its parlor his dining room, he was careful to preserve many of its original eighteenth-century features, including a hand-carved dining room mantel, the woodwork and moldings, and the central hall's double batten doors. The beautiful southern yellow pine paneling in the library was created from floorboards taken from the home's original attic.

Over the next forty years, Glass, along with R. Lee Taylor, created Glen Burnie's extraordinary gardens, which are composed of many unique components. An enchanting Chinese garden—featuring a pagoda, a moon gate, and a winding stone canal—and a water garden with a trout-filled pond are two favorites. The spectacular rose gardens contain nearly four hundred rose bushes, planted in beds and along brick pathways. Other spaces include the Pleached Allée, whose flowering crabapples are exquisite in early spring; the Pink Pavilion, which faces a sunken courtyard with an Italian fountain; perennial and statue gardens; a knot garden; boxwood parterres; and a formal vegetable garden. Strolling leisurely through the 6 acres of gardens is a joy, with something in bloom from spring through fall. The gardens are surrounded by 250 acres from James Wood's original land grant. Still in agricultural use, the rolling farmland helps this city property retain the ambiance of a country estate.

Before he died in 1992, Julian Wood Glass Jr. formed the Glass–Glen Burnie Foundation, whose purpose was to create a museum complex at the site. A local nonprofit corporation opened the house and gardens to the public in 1997. The first floor of the house is presented today just as it was enjoyed by Julian Glass, filled with his remarkable collection of antiques, decorative objects, and artwork.

The Glen Burnie Historic House and its surrounding gardens are now part of the Museum of the Shenandoah Valley campus. In 2005, a museum designed by renowned architect Michael Graves opened on the property, transforming the site into a regional history museum complex. This impressive museum, which showcases the art, history, and culture of the Shenandoah Valley, is open year round, while the house and gardens are open March through November (closed Mondays).

FACING PAGE: *Robert Wood began the original portion of the Glen Burnie Historic House in 1794. More than 160 years later, the last family member to own the property, Julian Wood Glass Jr., transformed it into a striking showplace filled with a fabulous collection of antiques and artwork. The mansion is surrounded by six acres of sumptuous gardens.*

ABOVE: *In Glen Burnie's gardens, the Pink Pavilion, featuring a bust of Hadrian over its door, looks out over a sunken courtyard that holds a splashing Italian fountain. Julian Wood Glass Jr. often used the furnished pavilion, which is equipped with a working fireplace, for entertaining.*

FACING PAGE, TOP: *The central hall, part of the original portion of the house, retains its eighteenth-century woodwork and double batten doors. The tall case clock is a Glass family heirloom that was made in Winchester in the 1700s.*

FACING PAGE, BOTTOM: *Julian Wood Glass Jr. turned the dining room of the original house into his library. The beautiful southern yellow pine that warms the room's walls, bookcases, and mantel was made from floorboards that Glass removed from the original home's attic. Glass' exquisite antiques and artwork fill the room.*

TOP: *Complete with a pagoda, a moon gate, an arched moon bridge, and a water-filled stone canal, the enchanting Chinese garden is one of the most picturesque of Glen Burnie's gardens.*

LEFT: *The interlaced branches of flowering crabapple trees form the stunning pleached allée, one of Glen Burnie's signature garden features. Glass and R. Lee Taylor designed and created the fabulous gardens over a forty-year period.*

Belle Grove Plantation

Belle Grove, the elegant eighteenth-century manor home of a once prosperous grain and livestock plantation in the northern Shenandoah Valley, has withstood the ravages of time, weather, and war and stands today virtually unchanged.

Completed in 1797, Belle Grove was built by Major Isaac Hite for his wife, Nelly Madison Hite, the sister of future president James Madison. Major Hite was a Revolutionary War veteran and the grandson of German immigrant Jost Hite, whose family became some of the valley's earliest settlers when they moved there from Pennsylvania in 1732.

Isaac and Nelly built their home on 483 acres given to them by Isaac's father. (By 1814, Isaac had expanded the plantation to more than 7,500 acres.) Nelly's brother, James Madison, played a major role in its design and called on his good friend, Thomas Jefferson, for advice on the plans. The new home was named Belle Grove, after the home of Nelly's maternal grandparents in Port Conway, Virginia.

The design of the original portion of the mansion is Federal with Classical Revival elements. The one-story, pavilion-style house has a raised English basement and contains seven rooms, including a library, day sitting room, parlor, dining room, plantation office, chamber, and nursery. Its 2-foot-thick walls are constructed of New Market limestone that was quarried on the property, and its hand-cut floors are 2-inch-thick pine. The home's interior, which includes both Georgian and Federal styles, boasts the finest hand-carved woodwork in its fireplace mantels and surrounds, friezes, pilasters, and cornices. Jefferson's influence is seen in such features as the T-shaped hall plan, the transoms, which help illuminate the home's interior, the lunette window over the front door, and the overall symmetry of the house's plan.

In 1802, just five years after moving into her lovely new home, Nelly died at the age of forty-two, leaving Isaac a widower with two children. The following year, he married twenty-one-year-old Ann Tunstall Maury, who would bear him ten more children. To better accommodate his rapidly growing family, he added a west wing to the mansion in 1815. The wing originally stood approximately 25 inches from the main house, attached by a passageway. Another addition in 1900 joined the two sections together.

Sold out of the Hite family in 1860, Belle Grove was appropriated by both the Union and Confederate armies during the Civil War. On October 19, 1864, the Battle of Cedar Creek, the last major battle of Union General Philip Sheridan's Valley Campaign, played out on the fields of the plantation, with the mansion serving as Union headquarters. Nearly 53,000 forces were engaged in the battle, which ended in a Union victory and marked the beginning of the end for the Confederacy. Remarkably, Belle Grove suffered little damage other than bullet marks on its columns and soldiers' graffiti on its attic walls.

After changing hands three more times, Belle Grove was purchased in 1907 by A. J. Brumback, whose son operated it as an inn. Dr. Francis Hunnewell, a frequent guest at the inn, recognized the property's historical significance. He purchased the property in 1929 and hired a preservation architect who sensitively restored the mansion to its early-nineteenth-century condition while carefully preserving its architectural integrity. Using Belle Grove inventories from 1836 and 1851, Hunnewell then filled the mansion with appropriate Shenandoah Valley antiques and furnishings.

Upon his death in 1964, Hunnewell bequeathed the mansion and 100 acres to the National Trust for Historic Preservation, which opened it to the public in 1967. While the National Trust owns the property, a nonprofit foundation, Belle Grove Inc., is responsible for its operation and funding. The property is open April through October and weekends in November.

In addition to the mansion, the site also includes original outbuildings, a slave cemetery, and a heritage apple orchard. A demonstration garden, designed by the Garden Club of Virginia, contains beds of early-nineteenth-century herbs, show crops, and berries, as well as a bed of cutting flowers from the period.

TOP: *Located near Middletown in the northern Shenandoah Valley, the elegant Belle Grove manor house was built in 1797 by Major Isaac Hite and his first wife, Nelly Madison Hite. The Federal-style residence was the centerpiece of what grew to be a thriving 7,500-acre grain and livestock plantation that also held flour and timber mills, a distillery, and a general store.*

LEFT: *Belle Grove features fine neoclassical carved woodwork in the public rooms of the house. In the parlor, rams' heads are carved into the capitals above the pilasters. Although ancient Greek or Roman in origin, the rams' heads at Belle Grove also represented the livestock grazing in the pastures.*

ABOVE: *Designed by the Garden Club of Virginia, Belle Grove's demonstration garden contains an assortment of early-nineteenth-century plants, including herbs used for cooking, scent, and medicinal purposes; show crops like flax and tobacco; and a bed of cutting flowers.*

FACING PAGE, TOP: *The golden yellow paint in the dining room was applied after an analysis revealed the colors used by the Hites in each room. The heart pine woodwork was painted to give the appearance of mahogany, a much more expensive wood. The carpeting here and in the parlor was selected based on Hite inventories that showed an order for rolls of Brussels weave carpet from England. An English mill made the reproductions.*

FACING PAGE, BOTTOM: *With its fine classical woodwork, brightly patterned carpeting, and plastered walls painted a beautiful shade of verdigris green, the parlor was the most formal room in the mansion. It is believed that Thomas Jefferson was responsible for the primary design of the room. Portraits on the walls are of Major Hite, Nelly Madison Hite with their son, James Madison Hite, and Nelly's mother, Nelly Conway Madison.*

The Woodrow Wilson Birthplace

18–24 NORTH COALTER STREET
STAUNTON, VA 24401

In 1845, Staunton Presbyterian Church of downtown Staunton decided to build a manse for the use of its ministers. It is believed that the Reverend Rufus W. Bailey, founder of Augusta Female Seminary (now Mary Baldwin College, located just across the street), may have designed the manse, since it is quite similar to that school's classical main building, which Rev. Bailey designed. The handsome, two-story, Greek Revival house was completed in 1847 at a total cost of $4,000. Built by local builder John Fifer, it features four rooms and a center hall on each floor, including the full, finished basement.

The Reverend Benjamin Mosby Smith and his family, the first residents of the manse, lived there for seven years. In March 1855, the Reverend Joseph Ruggles Wilson, his wife, Jessie Woodrow Wilson, and their two daughters became the second family to occupy the manse. On December 28, 1856, the Wilsons welcomed their third child while living in the manse. They named their new son Thomas Woodrow, after his maternal grandfather. He went by the name Tommy until he entered law school many years later, at which time he preferred to be called Woodrow.

Joseph Wilson was so successful in his service at the Staunton church that he was soon called to pastor a larger church in Augusta, Georgia. Saddened by his departure, the congregation bid farewell to Rev. Wilson and his family in early 1858.

After attending Princeton University, the University of Virginia Law School, and Johns Hopkins University, Woodrow Wilson spent most of the next twenty-five years in an academic career, first as a professor and then as president of Princeton. He then turned to politics, serving first as governor of New Jersey before being elected to two terms as the twenty-eighth president of the United States, an office he held from 1913 to 1921.

After the Wilsons left Staunton, four more ministers' families occupied the manse between 1858 and 1929. During that time, extensive remodeling and updating changed the house's appearance dramatically, and the red brick exterior was painted white.

In 1925, the year after Wilson's death, Mary Baldwin College trustees bought the manse from the church with the eventual goal of creating a memorial to the president. The Woodrow Wilson Birthplace Foundation Inc., chartered in 1938, purchased the house from the college. Restoration work, begun in 1940, removed most of the features that had been added during previous renovations. A restoration and preservation feasibility study in 1977 led to further restorations. Based on scientific analysis of paint samples, the manse's woodwork was repainted in its original colors. Period-appropriate fabrics, carpets, and wallpapers were installed, and in 2005, the white paint was removed from the exterior, returning the manse to the original red brick. The house, now completely restored to its 1856 appearance, includes many Wilson family pieces, including the president's birth bed.

The birthplace, which is open daily, is part of a complex that includes the Woodrow Wilson Presidential Library and a museum, which houses President Wilson's 1919 Pierce-Arrow limousine. The complex's lovely Victorian gardens, which have evolved in phases over the years, were one of the early restoration projects of the Garden Club of Virginia and were designed by well-known Richmond landscape architect Charles Gillette in 1933. The yard included only outbuildings and functional plantings during the Wilsons' residency, so the restored gardens reflect a Victorian design appropriate to the date of the house's construction. The plan features two terraces, the lower of which contains a boxwood bowknot parterre as its focal point. In the 1960s, a new brick terrace was added. In the 1990s, a forecourt and lawn around the museum were added, as well as garden walkways that connect the museum to the rest of the grounds. In 2008, the club planted new boxwoods and added additional perennials and hostas.

FACING PAGE: *The west front of Woodrow Wilson's Birthplace, with its elegant three-story portico, looks particularly lovely in the spring when framed by lush cherry blossoms. The birthplace is part of a complex that also includes terraced Victorian gardens, the Woodrow Wilson Presidential Library, and a museum.*

LEFT: *The bedroom in which Thomas Woodrow Wilson was born on December 28, 1856—"at 12 3/4 o'clock at night," as noted by his father in the family bible—is furnished with the actual birth bed and little "Tommy's" crib.*

Smithfield Plantation

1000 SMITHFIELD PLANTATION ROAD
BLACKSBURG, VIRGINIA 24060

Colonel William Preston was a Scotch-Irish emigrant from Ulster, Ireland, who went on to become a Revolutionary War patriot, county surveyor, and member of the Virginia House of Burgesses. In 1774, the wealthy landowner moved his wife, Susanna Smith Preston, and their seven children (plus an eighth on the way) to plantation land he owned in the backcountry of southwest Virginia in present-day Blacksburg. Here he built a fine home, named Smithfield in honor of his wife, and set about making his plantation a prosperous enterprise.

In his political positions, Preston made frequent trips to Williamsburg. Influenced by the architecture and furnishings he saw there, he envisioned Smithfield as a western extension of that same culture. The sophisticated, two-story, framed timber home, with eight rooms, a central passage, and a full basement with winter kitchen, was an anomaly in this remote Virginia backcountry, where log cabins were still the norm. Built in the Tidewater Plantation style, its glazed transom windows, raised-panel wainscoting, and Chinese Chippendale staircase were features typical of upper-class eastern Virginia homes. It is believed that the impressive fireplace surround in the drawing room was copied from the Raleigh Tavern in Williamsburg.

For the Prestons, life in this remote area on the western edge of the American frontier was perilous. In his powerful position as county surveyor, Preston expanded American colonization further westward onto Native American lands. He was also a passionate proponent of the American Revolution, and he worked diligently recruiting soldiers and acquiring arms and provisions for fighting both the British and the Indians. Consequently, the Prestons were vulnerable to attacks from neighboring Tory loyalists as well as disgruntled Shawnees and Cherokees. Governor Patrick Henry ordered a garrison of soldiers for the protection of Smithfield, which was surrounded by a stockade fence.

Colonel Preston died in 1783, leaving Susanna a widow with ten of their twelve children still at home. His will left her the use of his plantations, slaves, and stock, provided that she did not remarry. Well educated for a woman of that day, Susanna successfully ran the plantation after her husband's death. She continued to live at Smithfield until she died in 1823.

James Patton Preston, who was the first Preston child born at Smithfield, inherited it upon his father's death. A War of 1812 veteran, James served in the Virginia House of Delegates and was a Virginia governor. His son, William Ballard Preston, who inherited Smithfield in 1843, served in the Virginia General Assembly and was Secretary of the Navy under President Zachary Taylor. Preston and Olin Institute, a Blacksburg college, was named for him. It was from this college that Virginia's largest university, Virginia Tech, eventually evolved, and today Smithfield sits adjacent to its sprawling campus.

William was the last of the Prestons to live at Smithfield, but it remained in the family until 1959. At that time, Jamie Preston Boulware Lamb, the great-great-granddaughter of Colonel Preston, donated the house and 4.5 acres to the Association for the Preservation of Virginia Antiquities (now APVA Preservation Virginia). APVA's Montgomery County Branch restored the house and opened it to the public in 1964. With very few exceptions, the house, which had no major changes made to the floor plan over the years, is original to the eighteenth century. It is decorated with fine eighteenth- and nineteenth-century furnishings.

The Garden Club of Virginia completed a restoration of Smithfield's landscape in 1984. A demonstration kitchen garden, enclosed by a weathered paling fence, was planted between the house and a reconstructed smokehouse. It holds a variety of authentic eighteenth-century plants, many of them mentioned in Preston family documents. Plantings include food crops as well as those used for flavoring, fragrance, healing, weaving, and dyeing. Although plants were usually selected at that time for their utilitarian purposes rather than ornamental, many plantings provided both. For instance, pretty black-eyed susans and hollyhocks were also used for dyes.

Smithfield, which now sits on 12.5 acres, is open for tours from April through the first week of December.

FACING PAGE: *Colonel William Preston built his sophisticated Tidewater Plantation–style house in the backcountry of southwestern Virginia in 1774. In addition to the house, the site includes a kitchen garden, a reconstructed smokehouse, and a weaver's cabin, which was built from the logs of an 1820s slave cabin located on land once a part of Smithfield.*

ABOVE: *Flamboyant daylilies put on a show in Smithfield's demonstration garden. The re-created garden, a project of the Garden Club of Virginia, features a display of eighteenth-century plantings, including vegetables, culinary and medicinal plants, plants used to make textiles, and ornamental plants.*

GLOSSARY OF TERMS

baluster: A pillar or column made of stone or wood that supports the handrail of a staircase or the coping of a parapet.

balustrade: A railing or coping, supported by a series of balusters.

beaufat: A built-in cupboard or closet for storing and displaying china and other tableware; pronounced "bow-fat."

bond (bricks): In bricklaying, the pattern in which bricks are laid or joined together. The bricks are set in rows, called courses. A brick laid with its long side exposed is a stretcher. A brick laid with its small end exposed is a header. In **English bond,** the bricks are laid in alternating courses of stretchers and headers. In the more decorative **Flemish bond,** each course consists of alternating stretchers and headers, so a header brick is surrounded on both sides, above, and below by stretcher bricks.

capital: In classical architecture, the decorative top or crowning portion of a column or pilaster, which conforms to one of the five classical orders: Doric, Tuscan, Ionic, Corinthian, or composite.

cornice: The decorative molding along the top of an interior wall where it meets the ceiling or on the exterior of a building where the wall meets the roof eaves.

fanlight: A semicircular or semi-elliptical window with bars that radiate out like the ribs of an open fan. Usually mounted over a doorway or another window.

Federal (or Federalist) style: The predominate architectural style in the United States after the Revolutionary War until approximately 1830. Referred to as Federal in the United States because of its association with the new American republic, it was also known as Adam style or Adamesque after the architectural style made popular in Great Britain by the Adams brothers of Scotland. Typical features include fanlights, Palladian windows, balustrades, spiral staircases, and oval-, circular-, and octagonal-shaped rooms.

frieze: A horizontal band typically ornamented with designs or carvings below the molding or cornice at the top of a wall or above windows and doorways.

Georgian style: The architectural style popular during the reigns of King George I through King George IV (1714–1830) in England. In America, Georgian was the predominate architectural style from the early 1700s until after the Revolutionary War. Typical characteristics include a symmetrical plan, square shape, large chimneys, steep or hipped roofs, and classical details inspired by Greek and Roman architecture.

Greek Revival style: The architectural style popular in the United States, particularly the South, between 1820 and 1890, based on classical elements of ancient Greece. Characterized by pedimented gables and large entry porches with tall square or rounded columns.

Italianate style: The architectural style popular during the Victorian era and inspired by Italian architecture. Part of the Picturesque Movement that began in England in the 1840s, it was the most popular house style in America during the late 1860s and 1870s. Characteristics include a low-pitched roof, wide overhanging eaves with ornamental brackets and cornices, cupolas, and tall narrow windows.

mansard: A type of roof that has two slopes on each of its four sides. The lower part is steeper than the upper part.

mullion: A vertical bar made of wood, stone, or metal that divides the panes of a window.

Palladian window: A window that is divided into three parts, with a large, usually arched center section flanked by two smaller sections. The name comes from Italian Renaissance architect Andrea Palladio.

parapet: A low protective wall that runs along the edge of a roof, terrace, balcony, or similar structure.

pediment: In classical architecture, a low-pitched gable, usually with a triangular or curved shape, on the front of a building or across a portico. Also used to describe similar-shaped decorative pieces used to crown doorways, windows, and fireplaces. In a **broken pediment,** the angled sides of the triangular-shaped pediment stop before the apex.

pergola: A garden structure consisting of a walkway covered by a trellis or latticework roof supported by posts or columns. It is typically covered with climbing plants, such as roses or vines.

pilaster: A rectangular column that projects only slightly out from a wall. Similar to a regular column, it contains a base and a capital ornamented in one of the five classical orders.

portico: A large porch that usually features a pediment roof supported by classical columns.

post-hole house: A house constructed on wooden earth-fast posts that are set in holes in the ground.

Queen Anne style: A Victorian-era architectural style popular in the United States from the 1880s to the early 1900s. Characterized by flamboyant and fanciful features including towers, spindles, turrets, brackets, gingerbread work, and wrap-around porches.

quoin: A stone or rectangular wood or brick piece that is used to decorate the corners of a building.

Romanesque style: A Victorian-era architectural style popular in the United States between 1870 and 1900. Characteristics of the style include stone exteriors, arches, towers, and parapets, giving the building a castle-like appearance.

strapwork: Ornamentation created by crossed or interlaced thin strips either applied or carved in plaster, wood, or stone and typically forming a geometric pattern. Often used on ceilings, panels, etc.

wainscot: Wood paneling applied to interior walls, especially the lower portion of a wall below the chair rail.

water table: A protruding course of brick around the perimeter of a building between the upper and ground floors that serves to direct water away from the building's foundation.

BIBLIOGRAPHY

Billings, Warren M. *Jamestown and the Founding of the Nation*. Gettysburg, PA: Thomas Publications, in association with Colonial National Historical Park and Eastern National Park and Monument Association.

Brown, Katherine L. *The Woodrow Wilson Birthplace*. 2nd ed. Staunton, VA: The Woodrow Wilson Birthplace Foundation Inc., 1991.

Brownell, Charles E., et al. *The Making of Virginia Architecture*. Charlottesville: University Press of Virginia, in association with Virginia Museum of Fine Arts, Richmond, 1992.

Bullock, Helen Duprey, and Terry B. Morton, eds. *Woodlawn Plantation*. Washington, DC: National Trust for Historic Preservation, n.d.

Chappell, Edward, et al. "History in Houses: Prestwould Near Clarksville, VA." *The Magazine Antiques*. January 1995: 156–173.

Dean, Catherine E. *Bacon's Castle*. Lawrenceburg, IN: The Creative Company, in association with APVA Preservation Virginia, 2005.

Edwards, Betsy Wells. *Virginia Country*. New York: Simon and Schuster, 1998.

Farrar, Emmie Ferguson. *Old Virginia Houses*. New York: American Legacy Press, 1957.

Farrar, Emmie Ferguson, and Emilee Hines. *Old Virginia Houses: The Piedmont*. Charlotte, VA: Delmar Publishing, 1975.

Favretti, Rudy J. *Gardens and Landscapes of Virginia*. Little Compton, RI: Fort Church Publishers, Inc., in association with the Garden Club of Virginia, 1993.

Fordney, Christopher R. *Long Branch: A Plantation House in Clarke County, Virginia*. Millwood, VA: Harry Z. Isaacs Foundation, 1995.

Gleason, David King. *Virginia Plantation Homes*. Baton Rouge: Louisiana State University Press, 1989.

Gontar, Cybele Trione. "Rediscovering James Madison's Montpelier." *The Magazine Antiques*. April 2007: 120–136.

Hardin, Pamela G. *Carlyle House*. Lawrenceburg, IN: The Creative Company, in association with the Northern Virginia Regional Park Authority, 1998.

Horn, Joan L. *Thomas Jefferson's Poplar Forest: A Private Place*. Forest, VA: The Corporation for Jefferson's Poplar Forest, 2002.

Kostyal, K. M. *Compass American Guides: Virginia*. 4th ed. New York: Compass American Guides, an imprint of Fodor's Travel Publications, 2004.

Masson, Kathryn. *Historic Houses of Virginia*. New York: Rizzoli International, 2006.

Rouse, Parke Jr., and Susan T. Burtch. *Berkeley Plantation and Hundred*. Williamsburg, VA: Williamsburg Publishing, 1980.

Smith, Julian. *Virginia Handbook*. Chico, CA: Moon Publications, 1999.

A Visitor's Guide to Belle Grove Plantation. Middletown, VA: Belle Grove, Inc., 2000.

Wall, Charles C., et al. *Mount Vernon: A Handbook*. Mount Vernon, VA: Mount Vernon Ladies' Association, 1985.

Wheary, Dale. "Maymont: Gilded Age Estate." *Maymont Notes*. No. 1. Richmond: Maymont Foundation, Fall 2001: 9–14.

Websites

Abram's Delight: www.winchesterhistory.org/abrams_delight.htm
Appomattox Manor: www.nps.gov/archive/pete/mahan/eduhistcpaxmnr.html
Bacon's Castle: www.apva.org/baconscastle
Belle Grove Plantation: www.bellegrove.org
Berkeley Plantation: www.berkeleyplantation.com
Carlyle House Historic Park: www.nvrpa.org/parks/carlylehouse
George Washington's Mount Vernon Estate & Gardens: www.mountvernon.org
Glen Burnie Historic House & Gardens: www.shenandoahmuseum.org
Gunston Hall Plantation: www.gunstonhall.org
Historic Kenmore: www.kenmore.org
Historic Long Branch: www.historiclongbranch.com
Historic Smithfield Plantation: www.smithfieldplantation.org; www.apva.org/smithfield
James Madison's Montpelier: www.montpelier.org
James Monroe's Ash Lawn–Highland: www.ashlawnhighland.org
John Marshall House: www.apva.org/marshall
Lee-Hall Mansion: www.leehall.org
Maymont: www.maymont.org
Mary Washington House: www.apva.org/marywashingtonhouse
National Park Service, National Register of Historic Places Travel Itinerary, James River Plantations: www.nps.gov/history/NR/travel/jamesriver
Oatlands Historic House & Gardens: www.oatlands.org
Point of Honor: www.pointofhonor.org
Scotchtown: www.apva.org/scotchtown
Shirley Plantation: www.shirleyplantation.com
Smith's Fort Plantation: www.apva.org/smithsfort
Stratford Hall Plantation: www.stratfordhall.org
Thomas Jefferson's Monticello: www.monticello.org
Thomas Jefferson's Poplar Forest: www.poplarforest.org
Woodlawn: www.woodlawn1805.org
Woodrow Wilson's Birthplace: www.woodrowwilson.org

RIGHT: *Jefferson's private suite of rooms at Monticello, called his "sanctum sanctorum" by one guest, included his bedchamber, study, bookroom, and greenhouse. Pictured here is the annex of the bookroom, separated from the study by an elegant arched doorway.*

INDEX

Adams, James, 13
Adams, John, 77
Adams, Robert, 13
Allen, Arthur, 12, 24–25
Allen, Arthur II, 22–25, 27
Allen, Arthur III, 24–26
Allen, Elizabeth, 24–26
Bacon, Nathaniel, 24–25
Bailey, Rufus W., 120
Barbour, James, 73
Biddle, Owen, 100
Braddock, Edward, 65–66
Brumback, A. J., 116
Buckland, William, 52
Burwell, Nathaniel, 106
Burwell, Robert Carter, 106–107
Burwell, Robert "King," 106
Butterfield, Daniel, 28
Cabell, Eliza, 100
Cabell, George, 100–101
Cabell, Sarah, 100
Cabell, William, 100
Carlyle, John, 64–67
Carlyle, Sarah, 66
Carter, Ann Hill, 12, 36–37, 40
Carter, Charles, 35–37
Carter, George, 68–70
Carter, George II, 69
Carter, Katherine, 69
Carter, Robert "King," 28, 68
Chiswell, Charles, 84
Chiswell, John, 84
Custis, Eleanor "Nelly" Parke,
   54–55, 63
Custis, John Parke, 54
Custis, Lorenzo, 55
Dandridge, Dorothea, 84
Daniel, William, 100
Diggs, Katharine Garland, 100
Dinsmore, James, 87
Dooley, James, 80–82
Dooley, Sallie, 80–82
duPont, Annie, 88–89
duPont, William, 87
Elizabeth I, 74
Emmett, Anne Eustis, 70
Eppes, Francis, 103
Eppes, Richard, 38
Eppes, Dr. Richard, 38–39
Eustis, Louise, 70
Eustis, William, 69–70
Fairfax, Sarah, 64
Fairfax, Thomas, 64, 112
Fairfax, William, 64
Faulcon, Ann, 22
Faulcon, Faulcon, 22
Faulcon, Nicholas, 22–23

Fifer, John, 120
Finley, Margaret Eustis, 70
Fleming, Vivian Minor, 48
Franklin, Benjamin, 94
Garrett, Alexander, 97
George III, 65
Gillette, Charles, 74–75, 88, 121
Gilliam, James R., Jr., 100
Glass, Julian Wood, Jr.,
   112–113, 115
Glass, Thomas, 112
Glass, William Wood, 112
Grant, Ulysses S., 38–39
Grayson, Elizabeth, 69
Hankins, John, 25
Harrison, Ann Carter, 28–29
Harrison, Benjamin, 28
Harrison, Benjamin III, 28, 30
Harrison, Benjamin IV, 28–29
Harrison, Benjamin V, 28, 30
Harrison, Benjamin VI, 28–30
Harrison, William Henry, 28, 30
Heflin, "Peck," 48
Henry, Patrick, 73, 84–85, 123
Henry, Richard, 40
Henry, Sarah, 84–85
Herbert, Sarah Carlyle, 66
Hertle, Mr. and Mrs. Louis, 52
Hester, Maria, 97
Hicks, William, 64
Hill, Edward III, 34–35
Hite, Isaac, 116–118
Hite, James Madison, 118
Hite, Nelly Madison, 116–118
Hite, Jost, 116
Hollingsworth, Abraham, 110
Hollingsworth, Annie, 111
Hollingsworth, David, 111
Hollingsworth, Isaac, 110–111
Hollingsworth, Jonah, 111
Hollingsworth, Jonah Isaac, 111
Hollingsworth, Mary, 111
Hollingsworth, Valentine, 110
Hubard, William James, 77
Hunnewell, Francis, 116
Hutchins, Stilson, 69
Ingalls, Rufus, 38
Isaacs, Harry Z., 107, 109
James I, 8
Jamieson, Grace, 28, 30
Jamieson, John, 28
Jamieson, Malcolm, 28, 30
Jefferson, Thomas, 6, 7, 9, 14, 29–
   30, 35, 50, 73, 86–87, 90–96,
   102–103, 116, 118, 127
Johns, Jay Winston, 97
Johnston, Joseph E., 20

Lafayette, marquis de, 94
Lafever, Minard, 106, 109
Lamb, Jamie Preston
   Boulware, 123
Latrobe, Benjamin Henry, 106
Lee, Duncan, 74
Lee, Hannah, 40
Lee, Henry "Light Horse Harry,"
   12, 37, 40, 58
Lee, Martha, 21
Lee, Matilda, 40
Lee, Philip Ludwell, 40
Lee, Richard Decauter, 20–21
Lee, Robert E., 12, 37, 40–41
Lee, Thomas, 40–41, 43
Levy, Uriah P., 92
Lewis, Betty Washington, 44–45,
   54, 60
Lewis, Fielding, 46–47
Lewis, John, 46
Lewis, Lawrence, 54–55
Lightfoot, Francis, 40
Lincoln, Abraham, 28
Macqueen, Shelia, 107
Madison, Ambrose, 86
Madison, Dolley Payne Todd,
   86–87
Madison, James, 7, 50,
   86–89, 116
Madison, James Sr., 86–87
Madison, Nelly Conway, 118
Madison, Payne, 86
Magruder, John B., 20–21
Marshall, John, 76–77, 79
Marshall, Mary Willis Ambler,
   76–77, 79
Mason, George, 50, 52–53
Massey, John, 97
Maury, Ann Tunstall, 116
McClellan, George B., 20, 28, 36
Monroe, Elizabeth, 96–97
Monroe, James, 96–99
Morgan, J. P., 80
Muto, 82
Neilson, John, 87
Nelson, Adelaide, 106–107, 109
Nelson, Hugh, Jr., 106, 109
Nelson, Hugh Mortimer,
   106–107, 109
Nelson, Philip, 106
Nelson, Sarah, 106
Norton, O. W., 28
Offley, Sarah, 16
Pain, William, 100
Palladio, Andrea, 13, 90, 125
Parris, Alexander, 73
Piccirilli, Attilio, 69

Pocahontas, 8
Polk, Charles Peale, 85
Powhatan, 8
Preston, James Patton, 132
Preston, Susanna Smith,
   122–123
Preston, William, 13, 122
Preston, William Ballard, 123
Robertson, Lelia Skipwith,
   104–105
Robinson, John, 84
Rockefeller, John D., 80
Rogers, Edgerton, 80
Rolfe, John, 8, 22
Rolfe, Thomas, 22
Scott, Marion duPont, 87
Sears, William Bernard, 52
Sheppard, John Mosby, 84
Sheridan, Philip, 116
Skipwith, Jean, 104–105
Skipwith, Peyton, 104–105
Smith, John, 8, 22–23
Smith, Benjamin Mosby, 120
Spotswood, Alexander, 11, 84
Stanley, Gov. and
   Mrs. Thomas, 74
Taylor, R. Lee, 113, 115
Taylor, Simon, 110–111
Taylor, Zachary, 123
Thornton, William, 54–55
Thoroughgood, Adam, 12, 16–19
Tyler, John, Sr., 73
Vanderbilt, Cornelius, 80
Warren, Walker, 25
Washington, Augustine, 44
Washington, Charles, 44
Washington, George, 6, 7, 9, 35,
   44–46, 50, 54–55, 58–64, 85,
   94, 96, 112
Washington, John, 58
Washington, Lawrence, 44, 58
Washington, Martha Dandridge
   Custis, 54, 60, 63
Washington, Mary Ball, 44–45
Washington, Samuel, 44
West, Sybil, 66
West, Thomas West (Baron De
   La Warr), 8, 34
William George, 66
Wilson, Jessie Woodrow, 120
Wilson, Joseph Ruggles, 120
Wilson, Woodrow, 120–121
Wood, James, 112–113
Wood, Kitty, 112
Wood, Mary, 112
Wood, Robert, 112–113